INVESTMENT ENTERPRISING DEVELOPMENT

R. Lee Evans

Table of Contents

THE EXTRAORDINARY INVESTMENT TRANSACTION ©

CHAPTER 1
GENERAL INTRODUCTION

AN INVESTMENT DISCOVERY

The Extraordinary Investment Transaction (EIT) in a specially designed Limited Partnership (LP) © is a particular investment, a one of a kind, that qualifies the risk, reward, and timing into a very strong high-ranking investment for a secured Cash Investor (CI). A unique legal and financial investment prototype in a LP has been originated to rescue property equities from foreclosure, for the full and complete financial benefit of the property owners. The LP/EIT for the first time ever, initiates an innovative pattern of operation that forms and produces an answer to a major foreclosure financial problem never accomplished before!

The word "foreclosure" for many people automatically has a negative connotation. The foundation of the LP/EIT fresh approach is a very positive attitude towards helping the property owner in foreclosure in a very positive way. The EIT rescues all the property equity from foreclosure for the owner's benefit and the entire equity grows in amount through LP investment profit sharing. Also, all financial and legal negative consequences of a foreclosure are eliminated for the CI. And there is no charge to the owner for the use of the intellectual plan or work provided to rescue the equity. In the case of the LP/EIT any negative assumption one might make because of its involvement with a foreclosure simply does not apply.

Every investor wants a low risk, high return in a timely manner with no management or legal responsibility, without question. Finding one is not so easy in an everyday standard foreclosure transaction because of the high ongoing financial commitment, personal management, and legal risk the investor must take on. None of these many high-risk involvements in an average everyday standard foreclosure investment simply do not exist for the CI in the LP/EIT.

In the LP an original very low-risk high-reward investment has been created for a secured Cash Investor (CI). A systematic arrangement of legal, financial, and safety positions for the CI earns an astute investor's attention. The unique LP/EIT structure arranged for the CI establishes a legally sound, financially controlled safe environment, with a high return timely investment.

The LP/EIT is a three-party real estate transaction between: A Property Owner (owner), A Secured Cash Investor (CI) and A Limited Partnership (LP) that has two types of limited partners investors. The owner in foreclosure who invests real estate by contributing a property in foreclosure with substantial equity to the LP is one type of investor. There is also a second secured Cash Investor. Each limited partner investor, the CI, and the owner, have an individual purpose and a different legal, financial, and investment standing in the LP/EIT.

The property with a pending foreclosure contributed to the LP by the property owner will be taken out of foreclosure immediately. Then the "foreclosure free property's" fee simple ownership title will be <u>pledged as the collateral</u> to the CI. The full fee simple absolute title includes all the property equity that will be the collateral for the CI's funds invested in the LP. The property owner taken out of foreclosure is turned into a limited partner "qualified cash investor" in the LP/EIT when the property is sold for full value by the LP.

A foreclosure property in financial trouble is the essential ingredient necessary to form and start the EIT investment opportunity. The CI in the EIT will not be investing in an ongoing foreclosure. Instead, the CI is only investing in the proposition that a foreclosure free property will be sold by a professional broker.

The CI is a limited partner investor secured with substantial collateral but does not participate in any LP investment or share in the LP profit. So, the CI in the LP/EIT is not really an investor per se. The CI simply earns a pre-agreed fixed amount of Bonus as a reward for providing the LP start-up operating funds. The one act for the CI is to invest capital on a secured safe basis to financially prime the start-up of a LP.

The CI startup capital invested:
♦ Starts LP operating with start-up money invested.
♦ Establishes a new Debt To Asset Ratio that produces LP operating cash liquidity and creates a low-risk investment.
♦ Immediately is used to cure the first LP property foreclosure.
♦ Establishes a Financial Support Plan in the LP.
♦ Insures loan(s) payments by the LP, if necessary.
♦ Changes an owner's property under "duress sale" into a LP full value sale.
♦ Allows enough time in the open market to sell the property.
♦ Creates money to rescue the first three foreclosure properties, one at a time.
♦ Provides fix-up and sale preparation cost.
♦ Establishes a financial encouragement for the CI to join the LP.

The unique combination of the legal, financial, and investment technology in the LP have never been created in any investment project or legal entity before. The same purpose, performance, and results of the LP have never been duplicated. The LP has "comprehensive language", "investment and legal construction" and "operational techniques". These are all parts of a unique investment operation working together that create original and exceptional results.

THE CASH INVESTOR'S (CI) ROLE

The CI invests start-up funds of $60,000 in the LP in return for a healthy Bonus reward in the form of a pre-agreed fixed Bonus amount. The Bonus is calculated at forty-two and one-half percent (42.5%) of the amount of capital invested by the CI. Sixty Thousand ($60,000) invested earns a Bonus of $25,500 in approximately one year. A maximum investment of $100,000 invested earns a Bonus of $42,500. The Bonus is preset and cannot go up or down!

The CI is providing start-up funds to the LP that are secured with "a pledge" of a fee simple absolute ownership title of property approved by the CI. The property ownership after it is taken out of foreclosure by the LP is the collateral pledged to secure the CI start-up funds. The LP using the CI funds invested will afford owners in dire need of a financial help a fair and honest answer to their foreclosure problem. After the owner's foreclosure is cured and the property is sold for full value, the owner can now continue in the LP/EIT as a limited partner "qualified investor".

Usually when capital is invested in a LP by an investor it is directly used to purchase land to build on or buildings to refurbish to increase the value, so profit can be earned. In the case of the LP the investor's start-up fund invested in the LP is only used for starting up expenses of the LP operation.

The CI startup funds have a great deal of effect on lowering the investor's risk in the EIT for the CI. The LP "Debt To Asset Ratio" improves with the cash increase from the CI funds invested and creates operating liquidity in and for the LP. A property fee simple absolute ownership title with substantial equity is one asset and the CI invested fund in the LP is the other liquid cash asset.

The CI funds are used to pay expenses required to take into the LP the first LP property and to cure the property pending foreclosure. Curing the foreclosure means that the property value is re-established at the full market value and now the total remaining equity in the property is worth saving. This is because the property is no longer in a

3

duress sale loss situation instead now it will be sold in an arm's length transaction that will attract the full value of the property.

The CI fund also allows the LP to create a "Financial Support Plan" that will make the monthly payments on the property, if necessary, until the property is sold. The fund making sure all the payments are made also allow enough time to sell the property at full value. The advantages created by adding CI start-up cash are critical, as the cash both re-establishes the property value and lowers the risk factor for the CI.

DETAILING ACTIONS IN THE LP

The CI has the right to choose first LP property that will act as collateral. Simply put the investor is naming the amount of collateral that the investment will provide by approving a qualified property, with an appropriate amount of equity. The amount of equity in the property acting as collateral is known though the appraisal and is higher than the amount of the CI capital invested. If it were not so the CI would not make the investment and would not approve the property as collateral. The collateral, the property's "fee ownership title" pledged is secured with a Performance Trust Deed recorded in favor of the CI, at the start of the LP.

The Pledge of a "property ownership taken out of foreclosure" with substantial equity is the collateral chosen by the CI. The LP offers the "pledge" of a foreclosure free property's fee simple absolute ownership title as instructed by the property owner in the LP Articles. The CI is not making a loan that normally is secured just by the equity in the property. The "property's fee simple absolute title of ownership" is offered as collateral to the CI that includes all the substantial equity in the property!

The CI is privileged by a system within the LP that provides two collateral items to protect the CI funds invested. The CI cash collateral increases with each LP property taken out of foreclosure and sold, because of the Priority Use Position (PUP) granted to the CI. Per the PUP the LP cash-on-hand, gained from LP property sales, must be expended before any CI money invested (the $60,000) can be used for any purpose other than to take more properties in foreclosure into the LP. So, in effect the LP cash on hand from each LP property sale also "acts" as additional collateral. The cash collateral protection increases with each property sale. Both LP property cash and the pledge of the property ownership both protect the CI.

The CI is paid with a new payment system in a LP . The CI is paid a pre-agreed fixed percentage of forty-two and a half percent (42.5%) of the CI capital invested as a Bonus

4

amount. The CI Bonus is earned for providing start-up funding for the LP and is paid when the LP completes three property sales. Estimated to take approximately one year. The Bonus is paid out of LP properties sold for full value, after there are taken out of foreclosure. The Bonus is paid initially out of three LP foreclosure free property sales and later reimbursed out of the investment profits of the LP.

For the CI in the LP investment profit sharing is not what happens. No profit share is paid to the CI, instead a fixed amount of Bonus is earned by the CI. The Bonus reward money is already existing in the form of equity in the property that will be sold by the LP. The property sale money provides an initial way to pay the CI the Bonus, the property sale money used by the LP will be paid back by the LP from profit later. The CI Bonus "reward money" is a LP expense and in the final analysis is paid from LP future gross profit. Notice the owner is getting help from a cash investor for free!

The CI is investing in a LP and owns a legal right as a limited partner to be paid a pre-agreed Bonus amount for providing the start-up funds. The CI is not sharing in the LP profits. The CI does absolutely nothing after the funds are invested and secured by substantial collateral. There is no management, no legal responsibility and there is no need ever to invest more funds after the initial amount invested by the CI. This transaction also provides that it is not possible for the CI to become involved in any foreclosure or bankruptcy that would affect the CI investment. It is a very safe, profitable, and timely investment for an investor.

The LP/EIT is a new valuable investor/investment model with a new purpose never achieved before, i.e., the LP can now solve a property owner's pending foreclosure and rescue all the equity in the property for the total benefit of the owner! The normal legal and financial risk investment concerns are uniquely addressed and made as low as possible in the LP/EIT. The investment structure establishes a very safe environment with a generous and timely pre-agreed fixed amount Bonus payment for the CI.

There never has been a way, delineated in a workable form, like this investment system before! Individual parts of a unique plan of operation working together create exceptional results. The same purpose and results of the EIT have never been duplicated. CI in the LP:
- ◆ CI funds are secured with two types of collateral cash and property ownership.
- ◆ The reward is a pre-agreed Bonus of $25,500 to $42,500 maximum.
- ◆ The timing to collect the Bonus reward is approximately one year.
- ◆ The Bonus grows larger and is earned quicker with re-investment.
- ◆ CI is secured with substantial collateral, more than invested amount.

- CI initial collateral increases after the investment starts.
- CI has two different contractual legal standings in the investment.
- CI has a financially secured, safe, and legally attractive investment.
- CI has an expense free investment.

AND

✓ There is no legal or management CI responsibility.

✓ There is no need for CI cash reserves ever.

✓ There is no involvement or reliance on a profit being made.

✓ There is no CI foreclosure or bankruptcy involvement possible.

✓ There is no CI legal collection problem necessary.

✓ There is no property trashing concern for the CI.

✓ There is no owner move out problem to concern the CI.

CI FEATURES PROVIDED IN THE LP

A special structured LP, a one of a kind, changes the risk, reward, and timing into a very strong investment unique structure for a CI. All the parties involved cooperate because of their individual interest and benefit that will be gained from the LP/EIT. The property owner, the investor, and many related businesses all receive substantial benefits. The CI's investment in the LP is sublime as it realizes and answers all the normal investment questions, desires, and concerns. Other real estate investments cannot achieve the same legal, financial and investment status that the LP can for a CI and the property owner.

- Secured investment with substantial collateral.
- Dual collateral that increases with property sales.
- Limited use of investor fund.
- Bonus pre-agreed and secured Bonus.
- Bonus paid from existing equities.
- Bonus acceleration plan.
- Short time for a large Bonus.
- No legal or management concerns.
- LP rescues all the owners' equity for the owners.
- LP pays the CI for the use of funds to solve the problem.
- LP shares profit with the property owner investors.
- LP does not charge owners for the use of time and intellectual property.

IN ALL RESPECTS THE INVESTOR IS PROTECTED

The CI:
- Funds Are Safe And Secure With Two Types Of Collateral, Cash, And Property.

6

- Has Two Different Legal Standings In The Investment.
- Reward Is Fixed At $25,500 Or As High As $42,500.
- Timing To Collect Is Approximately One Year.
- Reward Can Grow Rapidly With Repeat Opportunities.
- Initial Collateral Increases After The Investment Starts.
- Has An Expense Free Investment.
- Has No Legal Or Management Responsibility.

CHAPTER 2
LP/EIT UNIQUE ANSWERS

ANSWER FOR PROPERTY OWNERS, INVESTORS & PROFESSIONALS

If a real estate broker or legal professional was asked, from an owner of property who cannot borrow money to cure an ongoing foreclosure, can you help me to avoid losing all my property equity built-up over years to foreclosure? The professional will have to answer, sorry if you cannot pay the default amount required in time, I know of no way for you to save your property equity from being lost. Now the LP/EIT changes the professional's answer to "yes I know of a way". <u>The LP/EIT can rescue 100% of the equity for you, without cost.</u> There is no other way in the general marketplace to help the owner rescue all (100%) of a substantial remaining equity in the property from foreclosure, the only way is through the LP/EIT.

With the EIT the property owner can now:
- Accomplish a full value sale.
- Maintain an investor status.
- Have all their equity rescued.
- Grow the rescued equity.
- Generate future purchasing power.
- Have the total loan balance paid off.
- Gain time to reorganize.
- Avoid long-term negative consequences that a foreclosure would create.
- Receive an expense free opportunity.

CI INVESTMENT QUESTIONS & ANSWERS

<u>The desire to be protected in a safe, rewarding, and timely investment is what the investor wants, needs and what the LP/EIT offers .</u> Here are the CI details:

- Question: what is the investment amount required?
- Answer: ($3,000 in group or single amount of $60,000 to $100,000)

- Question: what is the reward?
- Answer: (pre-agreed fixed amount of $25,500 up to $42,500)

- Question: what is the timing of investment?
- Answer: (estimated one year)

- Question: amount of investor protection?

- Answer: (property "fee ownership" is the collateral, equity exceeds invested amount)

- Question: security?
- Answer: (substantial collateral with superior duel legal standing)

- Question: source of reward?
- Answer: (owner property sale initially produces reward)

- Question: one-time Bonus payment?
- Answer: (no investment required to pay investor Bonus)

- Question: re-investment opportunity?
- Answer: (timing and reward increase substantially)

- Question: investor personal time?
- Answer: (no legal or management involvement)

- Question: investment manager?
- Answer: (LP)

A PERFORMANCE TRUST DEED (PTD)

The PTD is a legal instrument that used in a different way in the LP. The PTD secures a pledge of a "fee simple absolute ownership title" to a "foreclosure free property" that has "a substantial equity". The property becomes the collateral for the CI invested fund. The CI receives a PTD from the LP that is recorded against the property to make the CI investment secure and financially safe. The advanced way the PTD is used in the LP/EIT to secure a pledge of property ownership versus how a standard trust deed is used is eye opening. In the LP/EIT there is a new approach to investing in a secured investment.

A PTD is not a different legal concept, however the PTD is used in a different way and for a different purpose in the LP/EIT. There are clear important benefits over the normal trust deed investment using the PTD this way in the LP/EIT. Here is a brief outline that points out some of the many improvements using the PTD in this manor over a regular Trust Deed investment.

#1 EARNING IMPROVEMENT
- ◆ Standard Deed of Trust Investment

Results vary in regular trust deed investment from single digit to double-digit returns. Potential negative variables occur that could cause a loss. The amount of return is unknown until completion.
- ◆ Major Distinction

This new Performance Trust Deed way offers a pre-agreed fixed amount of $25,500 up to $42,500 in approximately one year. The same potential negative variables in a regular trust deed investment are not possible in this PTD Investment.

#2 COLLATERAL IMPROVEMENT
- ◆ Standard Deed of Trust Investment

Only a share of the property equity protects the new loaned funds of an investor. If the owner does not pay the monthly payments the property equity total can diminish by the amount not paid very rapidly. And a foreclosure if started becomes a serious time, money, and legal problem for the investor.
- ◆ Major Distinction

The collateral given to the investor in the EIT far exceeds the amount that a typical trust deed investment offers. Any loss that could happen in regular trust deed investment is not possible in the EIT because of the legal structure and the amount of the collateral pledged cannot go down.

#3 INVESTMENT TIME IMPROVEMENT
- ◆ Standard Deed of Trust Investment

The average length of a loan secured by a trust deed is three to five years.
- ◆ Major Distinction

This PTD investment timing is approximately one (1) year or less. Note: The timing can be shortened further with repeat investment and would also increases the amount of the investor's reward.

#4 FORECLOSURE/BANKRUPTCY IMPROVEMENT
- ◆ Standard Deed of Trust Investment

The borrower's nonpayment could create legal problems such as foreclosure or bankruptcy for the investor/lender in a second loan granted. This is costly and would severely diminish the investor's return.

◆ Major Distinction

In the EIT Performance Trust Deed legal scenario. a foreclosure or bankruptcy that would cost the investor time and money cannot happen to the CI.

<u>The PTD features for the investor are many and valuable</u>. The safety, reward and timing differences between regular trust deed investing and this PTD are very significant and are more attractive, secure, and rewarding. The CI receives a PTD from the LP and is recorded against the property. The PTD is the legal standing that secures the CI funds invested in the LP.

CI INVESTMENT CONCERNS ARE ANSWERED

The most important relationship in an investment is the risk factor vs the amount of reward. The smaller the risk the smaller the return. The bigger the risk the higher the return (called gambling). These are general principles that are hard to argue with. When making an investment the critical factors to be measured are risk, reward, timing, and business structure.

THE CI:

◆ Must be separated with two legal classes of limited partners so a qualified CI can invest safely in the same LP with a currently insolvent property investor! The two classes are completely different from one another and have different reasons for investing, different contributions, different legal and financial standings, different degree of risk, different system of reward, and different timing. The CI has his/her own limited partner legal, financial, investment standings in the LP. The CI has a separate class position that has no legal or financial entanglement with other financially insolvent limited partners. The CI is free of the worry of the financially troubled property owner limited partner having to direct any activities in any way for the LP. The General Partner alone has Power of Attorney in the Articles of Partnership and is authorized for making all LP operating decisions.

◆ Must be legally separated from the financially insolvent property owner in the LP. A Performance Trust Deed (PTD) secures the pledge of a fee simple absolute property ownership title as collateral, and this makes the CI investment into a secured Trust Deed Investment. This is an additional legal standing from the Articles of Partnership Agreement. Both the PTD and the legally binding Articles of Partnership Agreement have strong individual legal rights and legal standing for the CI.

◆ Must be in a secured investment position immediately. The CI invested funds are never without collateral as the Bare Title to the property from the property owner to the LP is deposited into escrow before the CI deposits the investment funds. The collateral for the CI is a "conditional pledge" of a "fee simple absolute ownership title" of the property, it is secured with a PTD from the LP holding the Bare Title and recorded by the escrow company.

◆ Must be extra safe with legal, financial and investment positions of advantage over other financially insolvent limited partners and is in the LP. The CI in the LP has no foreclosure, bankruptcy, legal or personal management concerns. In a it is a fact that the limited partner is legally limited to losing their capital amount invested. However, the CI loss of capital means the CI gains a title to the property ownership with sufficient equity to make up any loss. All these facts are established for the CI in the Articles of Partnership.

◆ Must be insulated. The LP is required under the Articles of Partnership Agreement to pass the property ownership title to the CI if the CI funds are exhausted without an LP sale occurring. The cash investor has the Articles of Partnership Agreement to claim and collect the title to the property through the court. In addition, the CI has a PTD to support a separate legal standing. The claim is based on the condition subsequent agreement spelled out in the Articles that says the property title is conditioned on a certain event occurring. Title to the property must be transferred immediately when CI funds are totally exhausted without a property sale occurring by the General Partner. There is no foreclosure or bankruptcy possible for the CI to be involved in.

◆ Must be paid on a different basis. A pre-agreed fixed amount secured Bonus is initially paid out of funds from the owner property sales. The LP then repays the Bonus as an operating expense out of gross profits earned from its investments.
  ▪ The CI Bonus is 42.5% of capital amount invested or $25,500 for $60,000 invested.
  ▪ The Bonus can increase in amount by reinvesting the $60,000 and the Bonus.
  ▪ The timing to collect the Bonus is approximately one year.
  ▪ There is no dependence on the LP having to earn profit to collect the Bonus.

◆ Must not be and is not concerned about the sale process because the subject property in foreclosure is taken into escrow and is cured by escrow. It is then listed for sale with a qualified broker. As far as the CI is concerned it is a simple property in and property out transaction completed by real estate professionals! The property owner limited partners in the LP, not the CI, must be concerned about the LP performance because the LP GP makes investment decisions using their rescued equity investment funds. The LP begins investing for profit after the CI leaves the LP.

♦ Must be free of any LP personal management. There is no requirement for any limited partner to perform any management task in the LP. The general limited partnership law requires that a limited partner shall have no management responsibility.

♦ Must be able to make an investment that is secured with the fewest problems possible in the shortest time and that earns a substantial reward. The LP/EIT does exactly that for the CI!

The CI has a unique safe and rewarding investment with all the concerns carefully addressed.
- ♦ The CI invests in a "secured transaction" in a LP!
- ♦ The CI funds invested have a Priority Use Position (PUP).
- ♦ The CI funds can be used only after all LP cash from property sales is used.
- ♦ The CI safety increases with each LP property sale because of the PUP.
- ♦ The CI is paid with a "new Bonus payment system" in LP/EIT.
- ♦ The CI is paid a "pre-agreed fixed 42.5% of capital invested" as a Bonus.
- ♦ The CI is "not involved" in any risky profit-making venture of the LP.
- ♦ The CI has two legal standings as a limited partner in the LP. The Articles Of Partnership and the Performance Trust Deed both have contractual legal standing that makes it possible to quickly collect the collateral, if necessary.

CHAPTER 3
FORECLOSURE PROPERTY OWNER SECTION

UNDERSTANDING FORECLOSURE

The technical meaning of the word is to wipe out a right of redemption on a property. Generally, this is what happens when someone does not pay his or her mortgage. Even though there have been no payments, the borrower retains an equitable right of redemption if, some day, he or she were able to find the money and try to exercise their right of redemption. To clear the title of this potential, a lender goes to court, demonstrates the default, requests that a date be set where the entire amount becomes payable after which, in the absence of payment, the lender is automatically relieved of the requirement to redeem the property back to the borrower; the debtor's right of redemption is said to be forever barred and foreclosed. This cancels all rights a borrower would have in the property and the property then belongs entirely to the lender, who is then free to possess or sell the property. The word is frequently used to generally refer to the lender's actions of repossessing and selling a property for default in mortgage payments.

In this writing a description of the property owner situation in foreclosure is put forward, along with a comprehensive answer, that expresses and embodies a favorable answer for the owners. The answer provides a property owner with the rescue of all their property equity from loss due to foreclosure and allows the rescued equity to substantially grow in amount. At the same time the answer eliminates entirely the all the painful negative financial and legal consequences a foreclosure would cause the owners.

In every business a service or product must be provided for the consumer to have a profitable business. A requirement to deliver a service or product to the consumer must be found before the business can earn income by delivering the consumer need, or by solving a problem. Elementary, of course, but every true. So it is in real estate, were a problem called foreclosure is a major problem for a great many property owners and businesses. A solution that will provide a much-needed fair and just answer to those in the foreclosure process is badly needed. The LP/EIT has the answer for the owner in foreclosure!

TIME IS THE PROPERTY OWNER'S PROBLEM

Limited time to perform. Under the foreclosure law, time to cure is limited to a very short time frame for the owner to find the money necessary to cure the foreclosure. The foreclosure problem starts for the owner when a Notice of Default is filed on the owner's property that has legal regulations designed to take the title from the owner. These regulations spell out the legal process and what rights the owner has, along with time limit for each step of the foreclosure. To cure the foreclosure, the time limit allowed to do so must be met by the owner or the property and equity will be lost.

The owner does not know the foreclosure procedure and the difficulties associated with the process. It takes time to learn this information, and this exasperates the problem by using up the little time allotted to cure the foreclosure. If time goes by without the problem being cured, it gets worse for the property owners. It leaves them vulnerable to a solution that is made under unbearable duress that will cause the loss of most or all their money.

The owner should know, but often does not realize, if contractual loan terms and conditions are not kept the process of foreclosure will begin! When terms of a loan contract are breached and a Notice of Default is filed, the immediate result for the owner becomes a series of problems such as: money, timing, low sale offers, and professional help difficulties. All these are serious problems for an owner to deal with to find an answer, within a limited time frame.

WHAT IS THE PROPERTY OWNER'S PROBLEM!

Money is the problem. The owner needs (money) to cure a pending foreclosure or lose the property with all its remaining equity. An owner in foreclosure has at risk all the remaining equity in the property to a foreclosure occurring. If the owner has a property worth around $300,000 market value and it is in the foreclosure process any equity in the property is at risk. The remaining equity amount in the property after selling expenses usually is about $70,000 to $80,000. That is a lot to lose for the average homeowner saving for retirement!

If we look at the market in the general marketplace, we see there are only two opportunities for the owner that are both unacceptable because the owner will suffer a great financial loss with either one. The first opportunity the owner has is to sell the property to a foreclosure speculator for less than the full value of the property. In this scenario the owner usually receives only a couple of thousand dollars for the entire $70,000 to $80,000 remaining equity.

The second opportunity the owner has is to just let the property go to foreclosure auction because there was no way to refinance the property and take it out of foreclosure. A foreclosure auction is generally a total loss as the bid price is usually what is owe on the property.

It is obvious that neither one of these situations are not really opportunities at all. The owner suffers a severe money loss and incurs other severe financial negative circumstances which are very expensive over many years.

THE CAUSE

Money problems of the owners cause foreclosure. The financial activity of the general economy influences the number of foreclosures, however some items causing foreclosures have nothing to do with the market conditions and will always go on and on. Some examples are divorce, drugs, death, poor money management, medical bills, college costs, accidents, bad business decisions, bad business market trends, employment displacement causing lower income, loan payment that are in flux: adjustable-rate loans, etc., etc., etc. You can see that when lenders grant a loan, they have no way of telling what might happen to a very qualified borrower as time goes on. Therefore, there will always be, without question, a very large number of foreclosures occurring each year throughout the USA.

ONLY WAY TO SAVE 100% OF THE PROPERTY EQUITY

There is only one way to rescue equity from foreclosure. Many claims are made to the effect that a foreclosure can be "solved" by negotiating with the lender or by filing a bankruptcy. Many books and tapes are sold making these claims. The truth is only one thing that will solve a foreclosure: **Money** is the only thing that will solve the problem and the LP/EIT arranges the money to cure the foreclosure and sell the property for full value!

Answer for the property owner. If a real estate broker or legal professional was asked, from an owner of property who cannot borrow money to cure an ongoing foreclosure, can you help me to avoid losing all my property equity built-up over years to foreclosure? The professional will have to answer, sorry if you cannot pay the default amount required in time, I know of no way for you to save your property equity from being lost. Now the LP/EIT changes the professional's answer to "yes I know of a way". The LP/EIT can rescue 100% of the equity for you, without cost.

With The LP/EIT The Owner Can Now

- ♦ Have the notice of default cured.
- ♦ Accomplish a full value sale.
- ♦ Maintain an investor status.
- ♦ Have all their equity rescued.
- ♦ Grow the rescued equity.

16

- ♦ Generate future purchasing power.
- ♦ Have the total loan balance(s) paid off.
- ♦ Gain time to reorganize.
- ♦ Avoid all the ugly financial and legal consequences that a foreclosure occurring creates.

There is no other way in the general marketplace to help the owner rescue all (100%) of a substantial remaining equity in the property from foreclosure, the only way is through the LP/EIT. A unique legal and financial investment prototype in a LP has been originated to rescue property equities from foreclosure, for the full and complete financial benefit of the property owners. The LP for the first time ever initiates an innovative pattern of operation that forms and produces an answer to a major foreclosure financial problem!

THE SCARY FORECLOSURE NOTICE OF DEFAULT

A pending foreclosure against property, if completed, cause the owner very serious legal and financial consequences. Such
as:

1. A loss of the entire equity remaining in the property.
2. A harsh long-term financing cost and credit damage because of a foreclosure.
3. A loss of investor status and future earnings.
4. A potential junior lender lawsuit after the foreclosure wipes out the lender's note.
5. A capital gain tax after foreclosure without the lost equity to pay the tax.
6. An owner needs to avoid all nasty foreclosure consequences by joining the LP.
7. A problem of no money, no credit, and a problem of earning the same amount of equity lost over again.

THE FORECLOSURE OWNER'S SITUATION

The owners in foreclosure are faced with many serious problems and must join LP or suffer serious consequences. The owner needs to solve all these serious problems, and only the LP/EIT can do it. The owner has:

- ♦ A mortgage payment is several months behind.
- ♦ No personal funds with which to cure the foreclosure.
- ♦ No borrowing is possible on the highly leveraged property.
- ♦ Personal credit disqualifies owner from borrowing more.
- ♦ Little time to find money to pay the loan arrearage and related costs.
- ♦ A long-term expensive financing problem due to a negative credit report.
- ♦ A capital gains tax if any is due after the foreclosure occurs.
- ♦ A tax with no equity because of foreclosure to cover payment of the tax.
- ♦ A collection lawsuit from a junior lender whose note was wiped out.

- A lack of ability to negotiate an "arms-length" fair price property sale.
- A lack of any solution in the marketplace that benefits the owner.
- No answer and no knowledge of how to rescue the equity.

THE OWNER NEEDS A LOT

The owner needs:

- To find a financial plan that can cure the foreclosure and rescue the equity.
- To find an infusion of cash immediately to cure a pending foreclosure at a time when the owner is financially insolvent and has no borrowing power.
- To immediately lower the owner's risk by curing the foreclosure.
- To gain time to restructure personal financial standing.
- To invest the money during the personal financial restructuring period.
- To eliminate the monthly payment and the loan principal.
- To retain equity and grow the equity for future purchasing power.
- To change a negative ongoing long-term credit problem.

The LP/EIT helps people in dire financial straits immediately eliminate the horror of foreclosure and gain control of their financial status. After becoming financially sound by avoiding foreclosure the owners can begin taking steps towards total financial recovery.

OWNER DETAILED BENEFITS

A legal and financial investment prototype in a LP has been realized, for the very first time, that will rescue property equities from foreclosure for the full and complete benefit of the property owners. The LP-EIT offers the owners an attractive foreclosure equity loss solution for the first-time ever! The EIT in the LP has the Owner in mind and:

- Cures the foreclosure through the LP.
- Sells the property at full market value.
- Rescues all the property equity.
- Shares LP profit.
- Increases owners financial standing.
- Avoids owner long term credit problem.
- Avoids any owner potential lender lawsuit.
- Gains time to re-establish owner's credit.
- Re-establishes an owner's investment status.

THE FORECLOSURE ANSWER

There now is a fair and honest answer in the LP/EIT to a century old foreclosure financial problem. The EIT in a LP is organized and operates in a profoundly unique

18

way. It solves a large segment of the foreclosure market that has never been addressed before with success. The need for this foreclosure answer is greatly needed.

Question? If you were the owner in the process of foreclosure looking for a money answer to save the property equity, would you join LP to achieve these benefits? The LP gives the owner a choice that would be difficult to say no too! The alternative is a giveaway sale or a forced sale at auction and would be devastating for the owner.

THE FORECLOSURE PROFIT SPECULATOR

If one would ask the question, how could a speculator buying for profit create a different financial way of achieving the same LP financial result for the owner? The numbers would make it clear; it is not possible for a speculator to offer the same 100% equity rescue. The speculator must take all or some of the equity from the owner and usually it is all the equity that is taken. Who would put up the capital required to cure the foreclosure and take all the legal and financial responsibility of ownership then share the equity with the owner? This does not make sense and history over centuries verifies that it does not happen! In the case of a property in foreclosure the amount offered to the owner usually equals the loan debt plus a few thousand dollars.

THE LP/EIT IS ORIGINAL

Question is the EIT something original or something that already exists that I know already? Answer: It is the latest answered developed to rescue the property owner with a pending foreclosure from severe financial loss! What the LP does not do:
1) Equity Sharing
2) Foreclosure speculating for profit
3) Short Sales
4) Flipping property in any way
5) Modification of the loan on the property
6) Any dishonest financial harm to owners in distress.

PROPERTY OWNER INVITATION

If an owner is in foreclosure and needs financial help to save the equity in the property and cannot find help, this letter sent to the owner provides a financial answer.
Dear Property Owner,
✐ A Foreclosure Is Sometimes A Difficult Money Problem To Solve.
The problem is that a foreclosure proceeding started with a Notice of Default puts the property equity at risk of loss if the money to pay and cure the Default is not found in time.

<u>Finding The Money</u> To Cure The Default Is The Best Answer.
Many owners after weeks of trying, realize that they are not able to borrow more money to cure the default in time. What are the options for the owner in this financial circumstance to save the property equity built-up over years?

<u>A Give Away Sale</u> Is Not An Acceptable Answer.
A very long history over decades of selling under financial duress caused by an ongoing foreclosure shows that a buyer will only offer a few dollars over what is owed on the property. The buyer pays almost nothing to the owner then immediately sells the property for full value and keeps all the owner's property equity! It does not have to happen!

<u>A Sale At Auction</u> Is Not An Acceptable Answer Either.
The lender's auctioneer is required by law to offer the bid sale price for what is owed on the property plus the cost of the foreclosure. A foreclosure auction generally results in a tremendous loss for the owner. The auction can be avoided!

<u>The Best Option</u> Is To Rescue All The Equity To Invest.
By joining LP/EIT the owner has the property foreclosure cured immediately and a full value sale is accomplished. In the program the owner becomes an investor using the equity rescued as investment capital and earns a profit share. All legal, financial, tax or credit problems a completed foreclosure would cause are completely avoided and owner gains time to financially reorganize. The owner's best option is to choose to save all the equity and avoid any negative financial consequences by joining the LP/EIT.

<u>Qualification To Join Is Automatic.</u>
There is no personal qualifying necessary! The amount of personal income employment status or credit score of the owner **does not matter**. The property by itself qualifies for the program no matter the amount of the owner's personal debt. An ongoing foreclosure or past bankruptcy does not matter. Timing is important so call for a free no obligation appointment.

In a no-cost interview the owner does not make a commitment to join. Written material explaining the LP/EIT is given to the owner to review. Only after a complete understanding is a decision to join made by the owner.

PROFESSIONAL HELP IS REQUIRED
When one understands how the LP/EIT works and what it does for the owner in foreclosure one could ask the question. What owner would refuse to participate in the

LP/EIT? No one would give up an opportunity to rescue $90,000 or $100,000 of his or her hard-earned equity and make it grow in lieu of losing the equity. And in addition, possibly be hit with long term legal and financial serious problems. Refusing the offer to participate in the LP/EIT means that the owner would have to submit to a forced sale at a foreclosure auction or a penny on the dollar sale to a speculator. The choice calls out to the owner to join or lose.

CHAPTER 4
LP/EIT DETAIL MONEY INFORMATION

LENDER'S MONEY POSITION

Lenders who loan money do not have a crystal ball. The lender can review a loan application very carefully. However, they will never know what will happen to the borrower that will change his or her financial standing in a negative way as time goes on. This is the reason the lender's judgment is good only for a moment in time. This phenomenon in the process causes many reversals of the owner's financial status that cause a foreclosure.

The institutional lenders such as Banks and Savings and Loans generally will not lend into a property that has a Notice of Default (NOD) recorded against it. No lender will lend money unless there is enough equity to cover the loan amount and expensive cost to collect because of a default.

A general rule is the *equity lender* will not lend money over seventy-five (75%) Loan to Value. The *equity lender* lending must qualify the borrower to the extent the borrower can pay the monthly debt service, before loaning more money. The owner is already financially overburdened as he/she cannot pay the current monthly loan amount.

REVIEWING THE NORMAL CIRCUMSTANCES OF A SECOND LOAN GRANTED

To understand the Extraordinary Investment Transaction let's first look at a junior loan invested in a real estate property. One would first look at the amount of equity, based on a qualified appraisal is remaining in the property, after a junior loan was granted. This is because if the junior loan granted goes into default, what would this do financially to the junior loan lender? Obviously, the dollar amount of arrearages from both the first and second loans in default would be subtracted from the balance of equity position. This would mean a new lower amount of equity protection for the lender. It would increase the risk of the loan considerably.

The equity lender would have to begin foreclosing on the second loan granted. This could take several months or even a year if the property owner filed a bankruptcy. More money is needed to keep both the first and second loans current. The costs of going to court to collect is more expense to the second loan lender. How much equity after the loans and all costs is there left?

The condition of the property could also be affected. The property maintenance could end up being expensive as the second lender would have to repair any damage to get the market price. When the second loan amount and all costs collected through a property sale how much did the lender make or lose?

BONUS MONEY PROVISIONS

Exceptional Way To Pay The CI Has Been Created As Follows:

- The "Bonus payment plan" pays a CI a pre-agreed fixed Bonus equal to 42.5% of the capital invested by the CI.
  - The Bonus is earned when CI funds are deposited, payment is paid after 3 sales.
  - The Bonus is a much higher percent yield than a normal trust deed investment.
  - The PTD ensures the return of the CI investment capital and Bonus promised.
  - The 42.5% is not an interest rate or rate of return, it is a lump sum Bonus payment for a one-time act of providing start-up funds to the LP.
  - Timing for the CI to collect is approximately one year.
  - The CI does not rely on the LP to perform any profit investments to be paid.
  - The minimum amount is $60,000, maximum amount is $100,000 to start an LP.
  - The minimum Bonus is $25,500, $42,500 when $100,000 starts an LP.
  - The Bonus is a pre-agreed fixed amount that cannot go-up or go-down.
  - The Bonus is paid out of funds from three of the owner's property sales, then the LP refunds the Bonus paid by the LP out of LP investment profits.
    - The LP acceleration plan increases the size and timing of the Bonus.
  - The amount of the Bonus can grow rapidly in each repeat opportunity.
  - A small investment amount by each member in a group can raise $60,000.

THE OPERATING AND INVESTMENT FUND (O&IF)

While helping owners with one of the most serious financial problems owners have, is indeed most gratifying, the LP main reason is to earn profit by creating an investment Operating and Investment Fund (O&IF) in each LP started. Because the LP can rescue equities from foreclosure to raise investment capital in large amounts quickly, the LP becomes a leader! Never has such an ability been developed to gather so much investment capital <u>on a never-ending ever-increasing basis.</u>

The LP/EIT is revolutionary. As a result of helping property owners avoid foreclosure and rescue their equity, the ability to build a new type of Operating & Investment Fund (O&IF) in a LP becomes possible. The O&IF size will accumulate exponentially, allowing for extremely safe and rewarding investments to be formulated. Rescuing equities from foreclosure to raise operating and investment capital in large amounts quickly is a first-time ever accomplishment!

All types of properties with owners that find themselves in financial difficulty, with no easy answer using normal institutional lending, can now turn to the LP for a financial answer. The LP O&IF will be able to invest for profit by financing the most difficult financial problem with backup up funds available.

The LP can raise millions of dollars of investment capital by helping property owners rescue their equity from foreclosure. When several individual LPs are operating, each one will gather investment capital rapidly. The O&IF will garner investment capital forever because a great many foreclosures will occur each year throughout the United States forever. This powerful way to gather large sums of investment capital is a considerable achievement.

Because of the Operating &Investment Fund, the financially trouble market includes the properties with a pending foreclosure and any financially distressed properties needing a money solution. The LP is not limited to just the foreclosure market. The EIT provides owners in any type of financial difficulty from land to income properties with a money source answer. The LP/EIT is a financial source for providing answers to many different real estate money problems.

A variety of new investment and financial opportunities are original and profitable because of the LP/EIT. Rescuing the owner's property equity using the LP/EIT can now help thousands of property owners in the United States with billions of dollars at risk because of a pending foreclosure! The LP/EIT truly is a concept based on an intellectual discovery that solves a serious problem for many people and businesses.

CI REINVESTING IN SEVERAL LP's

	Amount Invested	Bonus	Total Bonus Earned	Timing to Complete Each Partnership
1st Partnership Completed	$60,000	$25,500	$25,500	Approximately One Year
2nd Partnership Completed	$85,500	$36,337	$61,837 in 2 years	Approximately One Year
3rd Partnership Completed	$100,000 maximum	$42,500	$104,337 in 3 years	Approximately One Year

After building a bonus total to $104,337 by completing 3 Limited Partnerships in 3 years, each new LP will start with a maximum of $100,000. Investing $100,000 for 10 years earns a bonus for each LP of $42,500 or $425,000.
$42,500 X 10 Years = $425,000.

NOTE: The CI can Joint Venture with the LP 50-50 with the LP provides low-cost financing because of the Limited Partnership's O&IF. The O&IF is a major advantage and makes for a very safe and rewarding opportunity for a CI.

CI RISK IS LOWERED WITH EACH LP PROPERTY SALE

The LP takes in one property at a time and arrange a full price sale for the owners. The risk factor adjustment for each sale is shown in this chart. Each LP property sale lowers the investment risk for the CI.

Property 1 - Gross Equity of $100,000 in property 1
Total = Cash & Equity of $160,000 secures CI $60.000

Property 2 - $60,000 is replenished from Property 1 sale
+ Property Gross Equity of $100,000 in Property 2
+ $70,000 Sale funds netted from Property 1 sale
Total = Cash and Equity of $230,000 secures CI $60,000

Property 3 - $60,000 replenished from Property 2 sale
+ Property Gross Equity of $100,000 in Property 3
+ $70,000 Sale funds netted from Property 1
+ $65,000 Sale funds netted from Property 2
Total = Cash and Equity of $295,000 secures CI $60,000

THE PERFORMANCE TIME AND NUMBERS ACCELERATE!

As each LP property sale is completed a new property is taken into the LP and processed for sale. Everything accelerates with sales made by the LP.
- The number of LP's starting up accelerates!
- The Bonus amount accelerates with re-investment!
- The cash on hand in the partnership accelerates!
- The number of property owners taken into the partnership accelerates!
- The Operating And Investment Fund amount accelerates!
- The number of CI Performance Trust Deeds accelerates!

OPEN MARKET WITH NO LIMITATION

The LP/EIT market is not limited to just the foreclosure market, or just to residential properties. The LP's ability to raise large amounts of operating and investment capital for the LP to invest, its main purpose, makes it possible to deal with a wide range of properties. The number all types of money problem properties in the USA is staggering.

The amount of all types, residential, commercial, retail, apartments, land etc. of properties on which a foreclosure Notice of Default is filed each year is in the thousands and thousands. There is always over a million foreclosures in the pipeline in the United States every year.

Only a few represent millions of dollars of lost property equity by the owners and businesses each year because of foreclosure! It only takes a few properties to qualify for the LP/EIT when compared to the number properties that have a pending foreclosure Notice of Default. The EIT in the LP can raise millions of dollars rescuing property rescue and investing it to earn profit for all involved. There are more than enough foreclosure properties each year to build a most proficient system of raising investment capital in the USA. The total number of foreclosures filed in all fifty states each year is extremely large indeed!

AVERAGE $300,000 PROPERTY RESCUE ESTIMATE

$300,000 + Appraised value
$180,000 - 60% LTV
$ 15,000 - NOD Late Payments 5% LTV
$105,000 + Gross Property Equity
$ 21,000 - 7% Selling Commission
$ 12,000 - Closing Costs
$ 72,000 + Net Equity to Rescue and Invest in the LP

A MILLION-DOLLAR PROPERTY NOTICE OF DEFAULT ESTIMATE

There is a saying, "the bigger they are the harder they fall". Many high-priced properties receive a Notice of Default recorded against them each year! How many million-dollar properties are they like this? The answer is an awful lot!

$1,000,000 + Appraised Property Value
$ 600,000 - 60% Loan Principal Balance
$ 50,000 - 05% NOD Late Payments & Foreclosure Costs
$ 350,000 +Gross Property Equity
$ 70,000 - 07% Sale Commission
$ 30,000 - Transferring Title to LP & Selling Closing Cost
_____
$ 250,000 + Owner Net Equity to Rescue and Invest in the LP

NOTE:

Depending on the amount and the owner's need the equity amount that will be invested in the LP can be negotiated. It is not necessary for the owner is some cases to invest

the whole amount of the equity rescued. Reason will prevail, helping the owner is the goal! With a million-dollar property and $250,000 in net equity the owner could
1) negotiate with a profit speculator so the owner could retain say half of the equity. Not a total loss,
2) but if they join the LP, THEY SAVE ALL THE EQUITY. If an owner will take half for him/herself, LP can agree to split the sale proceeds in half. One-half cash out of the sale escrow for the owner and one-half invested in the LP! Different situations require different answers.

REPLENISHMENT OF CI FUNDS OUT OF LP PROPERTY SALES.

The Critical Cash Capital Fund is the CI's amount invested in the LP. It is used by the LP and replenished. The CI investment fund is replenished after each LP property sale as follows.

STEP 1: PROPERTY FINANCIAL STATUS
L1) $321,000 APPRAISAL VALUE & SALE PRICE BOTH
L2) $ 9,600 Minus Loan Arrearage (FUND MONEY USED)
L3) $215,070 Minus All Loan Amounts
L4) $ 96,330 ESTIMATE OF "GROSS" EQUITY

STEP 2: ESTIMATE OF QWNER'S "NET EQUITY"
L5) $ 96,330 AVAILABLE GROSS EQUITY (L4)
L6) $ 22,470 Minus 6% Broker Commission +1% For Listing Work
L7) $ 3,000 Minus Sales Preparation (FUND MONEY USED)
L8) $ 4,000 Minus Title Transfer Cost To LP (FUND MONEY USED)
L9) $ 66,860 BALANCE IS NET EQUITY AFTER SALE

STEP 3: ACTUAL SALE OF THE PROPERTY TO A NEW BUYER
L10) $105,930 SALE GROSS EQUITY (L2 plus L4)
L11) $ 4,000 Minus Sales Closing Costs (Directly From Sale Proceeds)
L12) $ 22470 Minus 7% Commission
L13) $ 16,600 Minus (FUND MONEY USED) Replenishment (L2 plus L7 plus L8)
L14) $ 62,860 NET PROPERTY EQUITY AFTER LP SALE

STEP 4: MONEY USED FROM THE CCC FUND IS REPLENISHED
$60,000 CCC fund
$ 9,600 Minus Loan Arrears (L2)
$ 3,000 Minus Sales Preparation (L7)
$ 4,000 Minus Title Transfer Cost To The LP (L8)

$43,400 The Balance After Expenses Paid Out Of The CCC Fund

$16,600 CCC fund is replenished out of the property sale proceeds.

$60,000 ORIGINAL FUND STARTING AMOUNT

LP CAPITAL ACCOUNT FOR OWNER AFTER SALE

$105,930 Gross Equity To Start

$ 43,070 Total Selling Expense (L11 + L12 + L13)

$ 62,860 Net Equity Equals Capital Account Balance

CHAPTER 5
OVERVIEW OF LP/EIT BENEFITS, ADVANTAGES, PROTECTIONS

LOOK WHAT THE CASH INVESTOR GAINS

The LP/EIT greatly improves investing in a new way that initially involves a property in foreclosure! The LP Identifies a new secured safe and highly rewarding investment in a very original way for a CI. Investing is much safer because of many CI protections and investment advancements granted in the LP to the CI. A qualified investor always wants looks for and needs a safe and rewarding investment like this one.

FORECLOSURE - BANKRUPTCY

No foreclosure or bankruptcy concern or expense can affect the LP CI. The CI collateral collection, if a LP default occurs, of the property fee simple absolute ownership cannot be stalled or involved in a foreclosure or a bankruptcy. According to the legal structure and terms arranged in the Articles of Partnership, the LP must turn over the title to the CI. The property title is automatically transfer from the LP to the CI.

CI CHOICE

The CI has the right to approve first LP property as collateral. Simply put the investor is naming the amount of collateral that the investment will provide by approving a qualified property. The collateral, the property equity amount is known at the start though the appraisal and is higher than the amount of the CI capital invested. If it were not so the CI would not make the investment and would not approve the property as collateral.

CI HAS TWO PROTECTIONS

The CI approves the property that will act as collateral and the LP cash on hand from each property sale also acts as additional collateral, so the cash collateral increases with each property sale. This is because the CI has a Priority Use Position (PUP) on LP cash, all LP cash that must be used before the CI fund is used for any other purpose other than taking in a property in foreclosure into the LP.

SUFFICENT AMOUNT INVESTED

No cash reserve is ever required for the investor to back up amount of invested funds. The investor funds invested have a limited use, if the funds are exhausted supporting the property without a property sale the property ownership title is given over to the CI automatically by the LP. There is no reason for the LP not to do so, as there would be not legal or financial benefit for the LP to hold the transfer of title!

LP IMMEDIATE REQUIREMENT

CI knows property will be up for sale immediately. Why because the Articles dictate that the property must be offered for sale immediately by the LP.

OWNER COMPLIENCE

The owner will leave the property upon sale when asked. The owner wants to complete the transaction to rescue all the equity. A penalty for not moving on time would lower the rescued amount by several thousand dollars.

PROPERTY CONDITION

No maintenance problem. Again, the owner wants the best price as is the usual case. Keeping the property in top condition by the owner is what will bring the best price.

CONFIRMING

CI has an ability to oversee spending of the CI funds invested by the LP. The CI funds invested must be spent on only allowed LP expenditures: To immediately cure the subject property foreclosure, to prepare the property for sale by the LP, to pay any escrow closing costs to transfer the title to the LP, to support the monthly loan(s) payments on the property, if necessary.

TIMING

CI's pre-agreed fixed amount of Bonus money is agreed to at the very start of the investment. The CI does not depend on any LP profit venture being successful or for the LP to pay the Bonus, the funds from three property sales are used to pay the bonus. The Bonus is safer and quicker in each LP reinvestment made by the CI. The timing for CI to collect is approximately one year.

REPAY

The CI investment money spent by the LP is replenished after each LP property sale before a new foreclosure property is taken into the LP. This creates a financial liquidity that lowers the investor risk for the CI and makes the investment acceptable to invest in for the CI.

INVESTMENT FACTORS IN THE LP

Security Plus:

Of paramount importance for the CI is the original way the LP is arranged for the first-time ever. LP cash and property fee ownership are both used to secure the funds. The security increases with each property sale by the LP. Securing an investor's collateral is critical along with a way to collect without involving the investor in a bankruptcy or foreclosure proceeding, in case of a default. The EIT provides the investor with a very positive answer that deals with and solves these concerns.

Loan Service:

The LP will service the debt when the owner cannot pay. Cash reserves are planned to make this happen. The property cannot go back into foreclosure because of non-payment of the loan before it is sold.

Legal Standing:

There are two contractual legal standings that make the CI legal position very strong to collect the collateral. The PTD and the Articles of Partnership.

Control Of Investment:

Control of funds and LP performance are under LP control.

Watching The CI Fund Expenditure:

The CI can verify the use of funds invested by the CI; spending use restriction is laid down in the Articles.

The Property Title:

The CI acquires the title <u>automatically</u> from the LP when the CI funds are exhausted without a property sale occurring.

Agreement To Sell:

The CI will see the property quickly put up for sale by the LP, as agreed in the AP.

Investment period:

The estimated time for the investor to participate is one year. Typically, other real estate investments take multiple years to complete.

Investment payoff:

The CI is paid a pre-agreed, fixed amount of 42.5% of invested capital as a Bonus. The payoff occurs when the third property is sold by the LP.

Avoidance Of Potential Problems:

The possibility of a foreclosure or bankruptcy interfering with the CI collection of the collateral does not exist in the legal structure of the LP/EIT.

Acceleration Opportunity:
The CI estimated one-year time to completion allows for repeat opportunities with increased security and lower risk. The CI can have multiple LPs funded at once and each working individually but simultaneously.

CI STRATEGIC ADVANTAGES

In the LP a remarkable investment for a CI limited partner is featured. A different and better way to invest in a LP that is very safe, rewarding, and timely is established for the CI. It has groundbreaking strategic legal, financial and investment structure incorporated.

In the LP the CI is offered a "dual collateral combination" consisting of (1) a contractual right, in the event of a default, to a "foreclosure free property" fee simple absolute title of ownership. (2) all LP cash on hand acts as collateral, which increases with every LP property sale because of the Priority Use Position (PUP) granted to the CI in the LP Articles of Partnership. The CI funds are legally secured and protected.

The CI has a very safe investment, regardless that it involves curing a pending foreclosure to start the investment. The property used as collateral is taken out of foreclosure to re-establish the full market value before it becomes the collateral. The CI is never involved in the investment without being secured with a "foreclosure free property ownership title"! The CI legal, financial, and investment structures in the LP are substantial improvements over standard limited partnerships . The reward is a pre-determined pre-agreed fixed amount that cannot go up or down in amount and is paid in approximately one year. The CI safety, reward, and financial legal structure offers the investor a solid first-time investment.

For instance:
(1) The CI is paid with a pre-agreed fixed amount Bonus of $25,500 to $42,000 in approximately one-year for investing start-up secured cash of $60,000 to $100,000.
(2) The CI is secured with a Performance Deed Of Trust (PTD) and a legal contract in the form of the LP Articles Of Partnership. Together they constitute a dual legal standing CI position that provides ultra-safety protection.
(3) Dual legal standing, dual colleterial, a new Bonus system, and a secured investment are all original in the LP EIT. These features constitute and offer a better legal, financial, and safe investment than everyday investments offer a cash investor.

Points In The LP for the CI are:
 ♦ Approves collateral and the CI funds invested are secured.

- Dual collateral is made up of a real property ownership title and LP cash.
- Is separate from property investors in all legal & financial respects in the LP.
- Is protected by all LP decision making away from owner.
- Avoids any possibility of bankruptcy or foreclosure involvement.
- Risk in the LP is lowered by establishing DAR cash reserves.
- Has a high return with no management or legal responsibility.
- Has a safe and secured investment featuring a substantial Bonus.
- Has an original Bonus payment system with a fixed Bonus payment.
- Has an acceleration plan opportunity that increases the Bonus.
- Has quick timing; three LP property sales and CI is paid.
- A favored legal, timing and reward position.
- Has a strong series of original investment protections.

The CI investment is revolutionary in original and profound ways. The safety, reward, and profit combination of opportunities in the LP/EIT are very attractive for the CI and are not equaled in any other type of LP. The CI legal standing in the LP/EIT is genuinely unique and provides a new degree of safety and financial reward for the CI, it also keeps the CI safe from any financial disappointment.

CI INVESTMENT SAFETY FEATURES
- There is no legal or management responsibility for the CI in the LP.
- The CI LP/EIT real estate investment is approximately one year.
- The CI will never be involved in any bankruptcy or foreclosure in the LP/EIT.
- The CI Bonus is initially paid out of LP property sales and reimbursed by the LP.
- The owner does not pay a dime for the help or money provided.
- The CI makes an investment in the LP that is secured with a property ownership.
- The CI will approve a property that has an equity greater than the amount invested.
- The CI funds are never without collateral as the bare title is deposited into escrow before the CI deposits funds.
- A Performance Trust Deed (PTD) is recorded against the property collateral that secures a pledge of property absolute fee simple ownership to the CI.
- The CI is always in a secured investment from the LP start.
- Pledge of property fee ownership title is the collateral.
- Defines all cash and property as collateral, creating a dual LP collateral system.
- Creates a system that maintains full equity and increases collateral.
- Has an easier and better legal system to collect the collateral.

- A new priority use position (PUP) defines first use of the LP capital and creates special accounting requirement for all capital expended.

UNIQUE LP SECURITY ACHIEVEMENTS
The LP/EIT provides:
- A way for the CI to pick and approve a property as collateral.
- A way to secure the CI collateral with a property title, not just the equity,
- A way to create CI dual collateral by including all LP cash as collateral,
- A way for the CI to check the financial activity of the LP,
- A way for the CI to be paid as agreed and on time,
- A way for the CI to verify the status of the LP collateral at any time,
- A method of increasing the CI collateral through LP sales.

SPECIAL STATUS
Seldom if ever does an investment offer so many positives for one investor in an investment. Each of these items favors the investor with strong and valuable features in the LP/EIT.

CI has:
- A CI very safe, quick, and rewarding investment.
- A pre-agreed fixed amount of bonus that cannot go down.
- A low-risk high-return CI investment position.
- A CI uniquely solid legal, financial and investment structure.
- A new system to collateralize and secure the CI.
- A new Financial Support Plan.
- A new Priority Use Position.
- A unique CI bonus payment system.
- A payment of Bonus and return of CI capital paid directly from escrow.
- A Bonus and return of the investment fund are CI controlled by the PTD.
- All investment CI concerns for the CI answered in the LP/EIT.

CI PIECE OF MIND
The CI invested fund is the Critical Cash Capital fund in the LP and creates:
- The Financial Support Plan within the LP, it allows the LP to start financially operating.
- New Debt To Asset Ratio creates liquidity and investor safety.
- No bankruptcy or foreclosure concern for the CI.
- Pre-agreed fixed amount of Bonus agreed to ensure large return.
- Payment of Bonus and return of CI capital paid directly from escrow.
- Payment of Bonus and return of invested funds is controlled by the PTD.

- Payment of Bonus is not dependent on LP making a profit by any LP investment.
- CI has a pre-agreed fixed amount of Bonus that cannot be changed.
- Return of capital and Bonus payment depended only on the sale of LP property.
- No CI cash reserve is required ever to protect the original amount invested.
- CI receives property reports (Appraisal, Contractor, And Preliminary Report).
- The Bonus plan in the LP, instituted for the very first time anywhere, allows the CI to accelerate the Bonus amount by turning over the funds from the last LP to the next.

CHAPTER 6
THE CI CATAGORTIES

CI DETAILS

- There is no legal or management responsibility for the CI.
- The CI timely real estate investment is approximately one year.
- The CI will never be involved in any bankruptcy or foreclosure of the property because of the LP collection system, that requires the LP to give over the collateral in case of a default.
- The Bonus is initially paid to the CI out of LP property sales and reimbursed out of LP gross profits.
- The property owner does not pay a dime for the help or money provided.

CI ACTION

- The CI makes an investment in the LP that is secured with a property that is taken out of foreclosure by the LP.
- The CI will pick and approve a property that will have an equity amount greater than the amount invested plus the Bonus promised.
- The CI funds are never without collateral as the Bare Title is deposited into escrow before the CI deposits funds.
- The Performance Trust Deed (PTD) is recorded against the property and secures the CI collateral.
- The PTD secures a conditional pledge of a property "fee simple absolute ownership title" for the CI.
- The CI has a secured investment in the escrow at every start of the LP.

CI EVENTS

- Pledge of property fee ownership is the collateral, not just a lien against the equity.
- The CI approves the collateral in the LP.
- All LP cash and property act as collateral, creating a dual collateral system within a LP.
- LP has a system that maintains the full property equity and increases collateral with LP sales.
- LP has an easier and better legal structure to collect the collateral.
- A new Priority Use Position defines LP use of the CI funds.
- LP creates special accounting requirement for all LP expenditures.

THE CI'S SIGNIFICANT PROTECTION STRUCTURES

- The limited partners separate class structure
- The Debt to Asset Ratio structure
- The property pledge acting as security structure
- The LP legal combination structure
- The use control of the invested fund structure
- The reward system structure
- The reward collection structure
- The timing structure
- The dual PTD and Articles legal standing structure
- The dual collateral structure
- The system to increase the collateral structure
- The bankruptcy and foreclosure avoidance structure
- The CI risk-reward structure.

INVESTMENT STATEMENT

- No investor status has ever been devised that allows an investor to invest safely in a way that helps an owner in foreclosure to rescue all their property equity for themselves until now.
- There is a combination of newly generated factors in a LP that, when put together, create a unique and safe way for the investor to participate in helping people rescue their equity.
- The CI investment is safe and earns a substantial reward at the same time.
- All legal and management responsibilities fall on the General Partner.
- A Low-risk high-return is what the CI receives with the legal and reward arrangements in the LP.
- The legal structure for the CI is the strongest possible from a risk-reward standing for a real estate investor in any LP.
- The way the EIT brings the owner together with the CI in the LP, in the same investment, is safe and is highly beneficial to both.
- The investment arrangement granted to the CI makes the investment a one-of-a-kind opportunity extremely difficult, if not impossible to equal.

MAJOR FIRST-TIME ADVANCEMENTS

CI Several Important Features Are:

- Do not have to risk investor capital in a risky partnership for profit venture.
- Separate account is created to confirm LP fund restricted use.
- Pre-agreed Bonus amount is earned immediately upon joining.
- Investor early return of funds allows for reinvestment.
- No request for additional capital will be required to protect original CI funds.
- No bankruptcy or foreclosure is possible for the CI to be involved in.
- Pre-agreed fixed amount of Bonus agreed to at the start of the LP.
- Payment of Bonus is dependent only on the sale of properties.
- Controlled spending of CI funds invested.
- A pre-agreed fixed amount as the Bonus.
- A collateral pledge of property ownership.
- A Priority Use Position to protect the collateral.
- A system that increases the collateral.
- An LP Bonus acceleration opportunity.
- No need cash reserves ever needed.
- No legal responsibility or management requirement.
- Reports on the first LP property (Appraisal, Contractor, And Preliminary Report).
- No maintenance problem as owner is in the LP/EIT as partner.
- Contractual control of property ownership if CI fund is exhausted by the LP.
- Performance is assured by the Performance Trust Deed given to the CI.
- No LP investment profit performance needed to pay the Bonus.
- Two CI legal contractual standings to protect the funds invested.

SUPERIOR INVESTMENT CHARACTERISTICS

- Limited partners separate class positions.
- Debt to asset ratio improvement.
- Collateral pledge acting as security.
- Use control of the invested fund.
- Reward payment and collection system.
- LP one year timing structure.
- Both PTD and Articles have legal standing.
- Dual collateral structure.
- System to increase the collateral.
- Bankruptcy and foreclosure avoidance.
- Normal partnership pitfalls avoidance.
- Low-Risk High-Reward investment

SPECIAL LP OFFERS A STRONG INVESTMENT

This Specially Designed LP Greatly Favors And Protects The CI:

- Provides CI professional reports used to analyze and approve property.
- Establishes CI secured investment with substantial collateral.
- Controls the CI cash that is used for the items that make the CI safe.
- Creates a LP Debt To Asset Ratio that provides extra safety for the CI.
- Commits to the CI a pre-agreed fixed amount of Bonus reward.
- Bonus is paid from existing property equities to be sold by the LP.
- Bonus reinvestment acceleration is available.
- Has no reliance on a LP profit being made to be paid the Bonus.
- Oversees limited use of CI investment fund.
- Amount of property equity acting as collateral will not decrease.
- Legally ensures the CI collateral will be available, if needed.
- Collateral increases with LP property sales.
- For the CI it means a foreclosure-free property fee simple title is the collateral.
- The collateral, the property equity amount is known at the start in the appraisal.
- There is a pre-agreed fixed reward limit of up to $42,500 in any one LP.
- Taking property out of foreclosure with the CI cash invested changes a duress sale into a full-price sale for the owner.
- The CI investment money spent out of the $60,000 fund spent is replenished out of each LP property sale before a new foreclosure property is taken into the LP.
- The CI collateral collection of the property fee simple absolute ownership by the CI from the LP cannot be stalled or involved in a foreclosure or bankruptcy.

HOW THE CI BECOMES AN INVESTOR IN AN LP/EIT

FIRST: The CI reviews a "Preliminary Understanding" writing that is not a legal contract. The writing just explains how the EIT works and briefly spells out the terms, conditions, and roles for each limited partner in the Articles of Partnership.

NEXT: When the Preliminary Understanding agreement is accepted by the owner, cash investor, and the General Partner of the LP, the General Partner then locates a property in foreclosure for the CI to approve. Three professional reports that deal with the property appraised value, physical condition and legal status are presented to the potential CI.

NEXT: The CI is the one deciding that the property will be good and sufficient collateral by approving the first property that will act as collateral for the CI funds invested. The CI will not invest unless the invested funds are secured with a foreclosure free property taken out of foreclosure, that has enough collateral (equity) to cover the amount invested.

NEXT: The CI then signs the LP Articles after the owner signs the Articles and deposits the property's Bare Title into escrow. Upon signing the CI becomes a limited partner. The Articles are a legal binding agreement with terms and conditions and is a blueprint for all the partners.

NEXT: The CI deposits the investment funds directly into escrow after the escrow receives the Bare Title to property from the owner. The escrow company cures the Notice of Default on the property chosen by the CI and the property is no longer in foreclosure. The CI will not give over any money to the escrow without the collateral security in place in the escrow!

NEXT: The CI receives a Performance Trust Deed from the LP delivered by the escrow company that is recorded against the property taken out of foreclosure to secure the funds invested. The CI is now a secured limited partner investor in the LP with the pledge of a property's fee simple absolute ownership title as collateral. <u>The value of the property becomes market value</u> again as the property is no longer in foreclosure subject to low offers.

NEXT: The first property is sold. The LP takes in a total of two more properties in foreclosure, one at a time, and sells them through a qualified broker. The CI signs off the first property Performance Trust Deed and will receive a Performance Trust Deed on second property taken into the LP. The CI waits for each property to sell to re-convey the PTD one at a time.

NEXT: When signing off the Performance Trust Deed (PTD) on the third property sold the CI collects back the capital invested along with the Bonus promised by the LP. The CI entire role in the EIT is receiving and then re-conveying the PTD when each LP sale is made. A sale of three appraised properties is what the CI waits for to collect the Bonus.

Notes:
After each of the first two property sales the money used from the CI money invested will be replenished, to the full amount, out of property sale proceeds. Each property taken in will have the full amount of CI invested funds available to take in and sell each property.

The money used from three property sales by the LP to pay the Bonus ($25,500) is replenished from gross profit earned by the LP. The three-property owner's capital account will be credited with the $25,500 the LP used to pay the CI Bonus.

A Low-Risk High-Return is what the CI receives according to the legal and reward system in the LP. The legal structure for the CI is the strongest risk-reward for a real estate investor in a LP. The way the LP brings the owner together with the CI, in the same investment, is safe and is highly beneficial to both. The investment structure granted to the CI makes the investment a one-of-a-kind opportunity. All legal and management responsibilities fall on the General Partner.

Investment statement
No investor status has ever been devised that allows an investor to invest safely in a way that helps an owner in foreclosure to rescue all their property equity for themselves until the LP/EIT. The list above is a combination of newly generated factors, when put together, create a unique and safe way for the investor to participate in helping people rescue their equity. The CI is indeed safe and earns a substantial reward.

DETAILING ESCROW COMPANY STEPS
Step 1.
An escrow is open with a qualified company. If the investor approves the property to be used as collateral the process for curing the foreclosure beings with the investor and the owner signing the LP Articles of Partnership. The Articles are the legal binding agreement that is a behavior blueprint for all partners in the LP.

Step 2.The property owner deposits the Bare Title to the property in foreclosure in favor of the LP into escrow. Then only after the escrow first receives the owner's Bare Title to property in foreclosure in favor of the LP does the investor deposit the investment funds into escrow.

Step 3.
The escrow company then cures the Notice of Default, and the property is no longer in foreclosure. At this point the property's full value is reestablished.

Step 4.
Then the escrow records a LP Performance Trust Deed in favor of the CI in the land record office against the property. **Note:** The CI now has a contractual legal position in the form of the Article of Partnership and in addition becomes a Performance Trust Deed secured investor.

Step 5.

<u>The first LP property is sold by the LP to a new purchaser</u>, and any monies used out of the CI funds to cure the foreclosure is replenished. The CI fund is replenished out of each LP property sale and is used to bring in another property.

Step 6.

<u>A second and third property is found and sold by the LP</u> and transferred through the escrow company to the new buyers. At the third property sale the escrow company returns the CI funds invested and pays the Bonus promised to the CI.

Step 7.

<u>The CI reinvests in a new LP</u> and earns a higher Bonus amount in a shorter time fame.

CI REASONS TO INVEST

Essential To Deciding To Invest Is A Review Of The Safety And Structure Of The Investment. This List Provides Just That.

- ♦ LP's new Debt To Asset Ratio creates investor safety.
- ♦ Three professional reports on properties.
- ♦ Do not have to risk investor capital in a LP profit venture investment.
- ♦ Separate account open for inspection to confirm restricted use.
- ♦ Pre-agreed fixed $25,500 Bonus amount is earned in about one year.
- ♦ No cash reserves required protecting the original CI investment.
- ♦ No bankruptcy or foreclosure concern for the CI.
- ♦ Pre-agreed fixed Bonus means an exact amount of return is known.
- ♦ Payment of Bonus is not dependent on the LP making a profit.
- ♦ Contractual control of property ownership if CI fund is exhausted.
- ♦ Payment of Bonus and return of capital is controlled by the PTD.

PROPERTY - LAW - MONEY- HUMAN BEHAVIOR

The LP/EIT addresses a century old foreclosure financial problem with a fair, honest, and legal answer. It solves a large segment of the foreclosure market that has never been addressed before with success. The need for the EIT is great and will go on well into the future.

- ♦ **THE FORECLOSURE LAW WILL ALWAYS BE!**
  The serious problem of foreclosure is fashioned in cement and will never change.

The laws regarding foreclosure are geared to legally recovering the lenders collateral (owner's property) in the case the loan is defaulted upon. If the loan is defaulted upon the lender <u>must foreclose and sell the property to recoup the funds loaned</u>.
THIS WILL NEVER CHANGE!

♦ **THE LENDER LENDING RULES ARE ABSOLUTELY NECESSARY!**
When the following facts are understood it will come clear that the need for the LP/EIT will go on forever. The institutional lenders such as Banks and Savings and Loans <u>generally will not lend</u> into a property that has a Notice of Default (NOD) recorded against it.

No lender will lend money <u>unless there is enough equity</u> to cover the loan amount and expensive cost to collect because of a default. Any loan granted from an *equity lender* must be protected. A general rule is the *equity lender* will not lend money over seventy-five (75%) Loan to Value. Also, the equity lender lending <u>must qualify the borrower</u> to the extent the borrower can pay the monthly debt service, before loaning more money.

The owner is already financially overburdened as he/she cannot pay the current monthly loan amount. Most owners in this situation cannot qualify for additional funds to cure the foreclosure.
THIS WILL NEVER CHANGE!

♦ **THE NUMBER OF FORECLOSURES WILL ALWAYS GROW!**
The number of foreclosures will always grow because the number of new properties built that could go into foreclosure in the future. Also, <u>there are a multiple of financial reasons</u> why an owner of property cannot pay the loan payment that cause the default. With these reasons one can see that there will forever be foreclosures occurring in the United States.
THIS WILL NEVER CHANGE!

♦ **A FORECLOSURE MARKET WILL ALWAYS EXIST!**
This is because the lenders who loan money do not have a crystal ball. The lender can review a loan application very carefully. However, they will never know what will happen to the borrower that will change his or her financial standing in a negative way as time goes on. This is the reason the <u>lender's judgment is good only for a moment in time</u>. This phenomenon is built into the process and cause many reversals of the owner's financial status that cause foreclosure.
THIS WILL NEVER CHANGE!

◆ THE NUMBERS ARE THE NUMBERS!

If one would ask the question, how could a speculator buying for profit create a different financial way of achieving the same LP/EIT financial result for the owner? The numbers would make it clear; it is not possible for a speculator to offer the same 100% equity rescue. <u>The speculator must take all or some of the equity from the owner and usually it is all the equity that is taken</u>. Who would put up the capital and take all the legal and financial responsibility of ownership and share the equity with the owner? This does not make sense and history over centuries verifies that it does not happen!

THIS WILL NEVER CHANGE!

◆ HUMAN NATURE CAUSES A MONEY PROBLEM!

No person whether a qualified new buyer or a foreclosure profit speculator will pay the full fair market value of the property in the process of being foreclosed. Everyone purchasing property for whatever reason always offers the lowest price to purchase the property. In the case of a financially depressed property in foreclosure the amount offered to the owner usually <u>equals the loan value plus a few thousand dollars</u>. This happens every day in the country.

THIS WILL NEVER CHANGE!

◆ THE EIT TRANSACTION ACCEPTANCE!

When one understands how the LP/EIT works and what it does for the owner in foreclosure one could ask the question. What owner would refuse to participate in the LP/EIT? No one would give up an opportunity to rescue all his or her hard-earned equity and make it grow in lieu of losing the equity. And in addition, possibly be hit with long term legal and financial serious problems. Refusing the offer to participate in the LP/EIT means that the owner would have to submit to a forced sale at a foreclosure auction or a penny on the dollar sale to a speculator.

THIS WILL NEVER CHANGE!

THE FINANCIALLY TROUBLED NATIONAL MARKET

In many cases the owner with a pending foreclosure has not been financially acting irresponsibly. Outside unavoidable forces are many times the cause of a foreclosure. There are many reasons a very large number of property owners go into foreclosure in the United States every year. Here are some of the reasons foreclosures occur: Divorce, drugs, death, college costs, poor money management, medical bills, bad business decisions, market trends, accidents, job loss, adjustable monthly payment increases.

Foreclosure is not only the owner's problem it is also a societal problem. Why because the process is unfair in that the financial punishment is so very severe. Purchase down payment and loss of years of supporting the property monthly payments to build up the equity nest egg for retirement is gone. Other nasty legal and financial consequences can badly hurt the property owner for years. Foreclosure is a devastating occurrence.

Many Owners, Lenders, Real Estate Brokers, and the Bankruptcy Courts can be helped by foreclosures being cured through the LP/EIT. A CI in the EIT earns a substantial Bonus by helping others while in a very secured beneficial investment environment. Real Estate Brokers can gain a "foreclosure free" 6% exclusive listing for finding and processing the owner and property. And each time a property is rescued everyone participating financially gains including and especially the property owner, lenders, and real estate brokers.

Not to be forgotten are the other properties that have financial difficulties other than being foreclosed upon. There are many different reasons why money is required to solve a property's financial problem. The reason LP can solve money problems for various type financially troubled properties is because of the "Operating And Investment Fund" (O&IF) created in the LP. The LP/EIT market it's not just foreclosures in trouble; it's all properties that need financial help to advance future positive performance. It works for foreclosures and all other types of financially challenged properties.

All types of properties with owners that find themselves in financial difficulty, with no easy answer using normal institutional lending, can now turn to the LP/EIT transaction for an answer. The LP Operating & Investment Fund (O&IF) will be able to finance the most difficult financial problem. These are all profit opportunities for the LP:
- ◆ Residential and Commercial Foreclosure Properties
- ◆ Single and Multiple Unit Income Properties
- ◆ Earthquake Retrofit Properties
- ◆ Brownfield Properties
- ◆ Negative Cash Flowing Investment Portfolio Properties
- ◆ Tax Problem Properties
- ◆ Fix-Up and Repair Run Down Properties
- ◆ Fire and Natural Disaster Properties
- ◆ High-Interest Rate Properties.
- ◆ All financially troubled properties are possible to help and improve to earn a profit for the LP.

Because the owner cannot finance a way out of foreclosure and cannot sell for the real value of the property the owner loses a great deal of money! <u>The total amount of money in foreclosure property equities that is loss each year in the United States is in the billions of dollars</u>. Now many of these dollars can be rescued and invested by the property owners to earn and grow the amount rescued. The LP is specifically designed and operates to cure a pending foreclosure to rescue all the property equity for the owner's benefit.

ALL TERRITORIES HAVE FINANCIAL NEEDS

- **Operating & Investment Fund (O&IF) Territory**

The foreclosure market is huge. The financial trouble market when considering all types of properties with different money difficulties is very large. The LP/EIT has a gigantic territory from which to help owners in financial troubled waters. Because of the LP's Operating & Investment Fund (O&IF) the LP can entertain all types of properties that have a money problem throughout the USA!

- **Investment Property Territory**

Where are the potential locations to build or buy real estate investment properties? Have you notice lately a piece of property in your territory whose time has come? Every day a need to develop a piece of property occurs in almost every territory. A person may not have the financial ability to buy and built. However, by joining in the LP/EIT one can contractually arrange for the financing to buy and develop property as an individual or as a LP JV partner.

- **Portfolio Problem Properties Territory**

Where are the portfolio problem properties located? The answer is everywhere in the entire United States. Investors who own multiple properties many times have borrowed heavily against one or two of the properties. This excessive borrowing creates a cash flow problem for the whole portfolio. An owner can now invest the negatively cash flowing property in the LP, as an investment. This avoids the owner having to a sell and dispose of the negative cash flow property without paying commission and transfer costs. There are millions of investment portfolios that need this adjustment in the United States to get back to a positive cash flow.

- **Brownfield, Earthquake, Fix Up Properties Territory**

Where are Brownfield properties needing clean up? Where is Earthquake damaged properties located? Many owners do not have the funds to do the work. If an owner has this type of problem in your territory the LP with the O&IF can help. The owner has a limited time to solve the problem, or the in many cases the property could be condemned.

These All Qualify For The LP/EIT.
Foreclosure Properties, Investment Portfolio Properties, Earthquake Retrofit Properties, Tax Problem Properties, Brownfield Properties, Any Property In Financial Difficulty.

LP OPERATES DIFFERENTLY

LAW

Never has there been an arrangement that divides the ownership of a property <u>for the purpose of curing a pending foreclosure and rescuing the property equity</u> in the same way the LP/EIT does it. A Bare Title is a "legal arrangement" that splits the (legal rights) and (the equitable interest) into two categories. One being the "actual title" to the property and the other is the "equitable interest" in the property. The owner retains the equitable rights until the property is sold by the holder of the Bare Title, the LP. The holder of the Bare Title having the legal title is the only one that can sell and transfer the ownership according to law and the LP Articles of Partnership.

FEE SIMPLE SUBJECT TO EXECUTORY LIMITATION

A fee simple subject to an executory limitation provides for the estate to pass to a third person (one other than the grantor) upon the happening of the stated event.

CAPITAL CONTRIBUTION INVESTMENT

Investing property is the same as investing money or any other type of asset. The value of any type of asset transferred as an investment becomes the cost basis for tax purposes. Any profit from the investment made beyond the initial basis is taxed when the CI makes and collects profit.

INVESTOR

Never in any investment has an investor had the same legal, financial and investment advantages as the CI does in the LP/EIT transaction. Never has an investor been legally and financially secured in a special way, without any personal management or liability, and paid with a pre-agreed fixed reward amount. The CI is safe, rewarded and protected from negative investment influences that cause financial harm in standard investments. It is a first-time investment structure with the investor's safety and protection in mind, and it has no rival.

FINANCE

Never has there been an investment that has such a great ability and upside to do so much for so many, that only requires a small amount of money to find and process foreclosure properties. The amount of money needed to start finding properties to process is minimal. The CI capital invested is operating capital and secured with substantial collateral and is all that is needed to start the LP.

MONEY

Never has there been a transfer of legal title, to cure a pending foreclosure, the way the EIT transaction does it. No money is passed to the owner for the title. No LP property loan is needed to pay for the title. The money received by the LP from the property sale has restricted use and accounting verification.

FORECLOSURE MARKET

Never has there been a way before the EIT for the owner to rescue 100% of property equity from being lost to a foreclosure. The general market just offers the owners who cannot paid the default amount two choices:
1) Sell at give-away-price or
2) Sell it a foreclosure auction usually for nothing.
This has happened repeatedly over many decades a million times. It has been proven and the amount of money lost by property owners is staggering.

TERRITORY

Never has there been an investment market as large as the foreclosure market coupled with the number of all types of properties needing a money answer. It is because foreclosure have gone on forever and will continue to do so. Millions of Notices of Defaults and bankruptcies involving real estate in the United States are ongoing in the pipeline all the time.

INTRODUCING LP SIGNIFICANT ACTIVITY

- A special agreement in the form of LP Articles was created.
- A capital contribution of a foreclosure property is used as an investment.
- A new way to create an investor secured transaction is achieved.
- A system that created dual collateral is established.
- A separation of limited partners is created with two classes of limited partners.
- A new use of Performance Trust Deed was established.
- A new use for a Bare Title was established.
- A new type of Financial Support Plan was established to finance the plan.
- A full sale rescue for foreclosure property was created.
- A default collection system for a cash investor was designed.
- A new Debt To Asset Ratio formula needed to be established.
- A way for limited partners to participate in a cooperative solution was created.

ORIGINAL LP TECHNIQUES FOR THE CI

CI's overview:

- Quick timing.
- Secured capital.
- Pre-agreed fixed amount of Bonus.
- Dual collateral for security.
- Collateral security increase.
- Two ways to be successful in one investment.
- LP sales pay the CI Bonus.
- Easy collection system.
- Investment acceleration plan.

CI MONEY CONSIDERATIONS

- Timing of CI investment accelerates, and the Bonus increases with re-investment.
- A Priority Use Position makes it a requirement that the LP use all its cash on hand before any of the CI fund money is used. This means the risk for the CI is less because the LP is lowering the drawdown of the CI amount invested.
- The owner will pay the loan payments to the extent that it is possible. A Financial Support Plan using the CI invested funds to support the property monthly loan payment(s) is possible, only if necessary. This will keep the property out of foreclosure until a sale occurs.
- The $60,000 invested by the CI has an expense spending limitation on items that it can be used for in the LP Articles Of Partnership. It states clearly that the CI funds cannot be used by the LP as venture capital or invested for profit.
- A separate LP accounting to ensure proper use of CI funds is made.
- The CI funds invested are secured.
- The CI approves collateral.
- CI dual collateral is a real estate property ownership pledge and LP cash on hand.
- CI is favored with legal, timing and reward original positions.
- The LP has a different CI payment system with a pre-agreed fixed Bonus.
- The LP lowers the CI risk in the LP by establishing a cash reserve plan.
- The LP grants the CI a high return, no management or legal responsibility.
- The CI has a re-investment acceleration opportunity.
- CI is separate from the financially insolvent owners in all respects.
- The CI has quick timing three LP sales and CI is paid.
- Protects CI by keeping all financial decision making away from owner.

- Avoids any possibility of a CI bankruptcy or foreclosure involvement.
- The CI safety increases with each LP property sale because of the PUP.
- The CI is paid with a "new Bonus payment system" in a LP.
- The CI can "accelerate and increase" the Bonus amount by reinvesting.

LP NEW DEBT TO ASSET RATIO

Creating "money" that improves the LP Debt to Asset Ratio (DAR). The LP DAR is changed and improved by the cash amount invested by the CI. The new DAR creates a financial situation that lowers and makes the CI investment risk factor acceptable. The percent of security goes up and the risk percentage goes down for the CI because of the CI funds invested in the LP. The CI can invest safely, and the LP can operate safely with the increase in operating cash invested by the CI.

The liquidity created by the CI cash invested plus the owners making the monthly payment, to the degree they can, are key ingredients for the financial maintenance of the property's value rescued from foreclosure. The cash invested by the CI is used to support the loan monthly payments for the mortgage on the property until it is sold, only if necessary. The CI cash protects the property acting as collateral from going back into foreclosure and maintains the full property value and the equity position in the property. The added CI cash is of sufficient size to support the property financially until it is sold for the owner's benefit. Liquidity is a necessary ingredient in any successful investment, and this is what the CI funds create in and for the LP.

The way the LP added cash is used that the CI invests makes all the difference! Taking property out of foreclosure with the CI cash changes a duress sale into a full value sale price for the owner. For the CI it means a "foreclosure free property absolute fee simple title of ownership" becomes the collateral. Very importantly the cash allows for time to sell the property for full value. The CI investment funds help make the LP investment an acceptable one for the CI.

The only allowed LP expenditures of the CI funds invested are:
- To immediately cure the subject property foreclosure.
- To prepare the property for sale by the LP.
- To pay escrow closing costs to transfer the title to the LP.
- To support the monthly loan(s) payments on the property, if necessary.
- To pay some specified limited LP operating expense.
- All CI invested monies spent by the LP are replenished after each LP property sale.

CI PRIORITY USE POSITION (PUP)

A "Priority Use Position" (PUP) is created in the Articles of Partnership. It establishes that all the LP cash on hand from a LP property sale must be spent by the LP, before any of the CI's replenished cash invested ($60,000) is used for any purpose. The fund is of sufficient size to complete what is required financially for the LP to cure the foreclosure and sell the property for full price for the owner's benefit.

The PUP creates a new type of dual collateral concept in a LP that favors the CI. All LP funds from LP property sales must be expended first and the CI invested money ($60,000) is held in reserve. This means after the first foreclosure property taken out of foreclosure is sold the sale proceeds become LP operating funds. After the first property sale proceeds come into the LP, some or all the CI invested funds will now be in reserve for the next property acquisition. This means the risk for the CI is less because the LP sale proceed is lowering the drawdown of the CI amount invested in the LP.

The CI approves the property that will act as collateral and the LP cash on hand from each property sale also acts as additional collateral. The other major collateral for the CI is the "pledge of fee simple absolute property ownership title". The LP/EIT creates:
- A way to approve the collateral amount for the CI.
- A way to secure the CI with a property title of ownership.
- A way to create CI dual collateral by including all LP cash as collateral.
- A way to increase the CI collateral through LP property sales.

LP FINANCIAL SUPPORT PLAN

The money invested by the CI creates a "Financial Support Plan" in the LP. The CI funds are given over on a secured basis to the LP, to cure a pending foreclosure on the property. We call the CI invested funds "Critical Cash Capital" (CCC) in the LP.

The funds invested by the CI has a limitation on what items the funds can be used for by the LP, spelled out in the Articles of Partnership. It states clearly that the CI funds cannot be used by the LP as venture capital or invested for a profit venture. A separate LP accounting to ensure proper use of CI funds is made for the CI to review. The only allowed LP expenditures of the CI funds invested are:
- To take into the LP three properties in foreclosure,
- To immediately cure a property foreclosure,
- To prepare the property taken out of foreclosure for sale by the LP,
- To pay any escrow closing costs to transfer the Bare Title to the LP,
- To support the monthly loan(s) payments on the property, if necessary,

- To pay some limited LP operating expense.

All CI invested monies spent by the LP are replenished out of the LP proceeds from LP property sales that were taken out of foreclosure. The CI fund acts as an operating fund only for the LP, it cannot be invested by the LP. The CCC fund may be used by the LP to financially support the loan payments on the property until it sells, if necessary. The liquidity created by the CI cash and the owners making the monthly payment (to the degree they can) are key financial supporting ingredients. This loan payment system maintains and solidifies the full equity position of the property until it is sold. It will also keep the property out of default until a sale occurs.

"LEGAL COMBINATION" IN THE LP

The "One And Only" Legal Combination That Will Work. This is the only original legal scenario that will work to avoid foreclosure and rescued the total property equity for the property owner's benefit. The LP "special legal arrangement" makes it possible; it would not work without this legal combination.

The combination:
- A unique LP and its original set of Articles Of Partnership,
- A Power Of Attorney that includes a special fiduciary relationship created,
- A Bare Title/Equitable Title division of ownership rights,
- A Grant Deed with special required terms,
- A use of Fee Simple Executory Limitation, a Determinable Fee,
- A securing of a pledge with a Performance Trust Deed, and
- A Condition Subsequent agreement to transfer and sell property.

In the LP EIT there are established legal statues in the Articles of Partnership for the LP that are seldom used in a real estate property transaction. Legal principals and laws used in the LP have never been used together in combination in a LP or investment of any type before. This is a unique legal arrangement that establishes a viable method to rescue 100% of the property equity for the owner. The LP legal structure also creates a new way for a qualified cash investor to invest safely! NOTE: The laws and principals are all statues and regulations in law! No made-up laws in the LP!

Without the unique comprehensive legal arrangement there would be no new type of investor providing money and no way to complete the purpose of the LP. It is the "LEGAL COMBINATION OF LEGAL STATUTES" that creates ability to perform the transaction. And no other such legal grouping for the purpose of saving property equity has ever been established before! Also, without this legal structure it would not be possible to raise large sums of "Operating and Investment Capital" on an ongoing never-ending repetitive basis to invest for profit.

Here are terms used in the LP that are unusual to the real estate community. Some of these legal statues and regulations are never used by real estate brokers in normal everyday sale activity. They are:

- A Special Individual Purpose Set Of Articles Of Partnership (AP).
- A Unique General Partner (GP) Power Of Attorney In The AP.
- A Special Use For A Performance Trust Deed (PTD).
- A Special Use Of The Bare Title Principal Of "Non-Possessory" Ownership. Definition: Bare Title is a type of non-possessory ownership. Bare title lacks the usual rights and privileges of ownership. A trustee or fiduciary in a deed of trust securing instrument may hold the title to a secured property but only such title as is needed to carry to the terms of the lien document (contract). The AP conditions the Grant Deed transfer to the Partnership with a Bare Title "Non-Possessory" position meaning the Partnership holds the property title only to sell and transfer the title on behalf of the owner to a new buyer. The Partnership will become the "holder on condition for disposition" for the property owner when it receives the Grant Deed from escrow. POSSESSION: The act or state of owning or holding something.
- A Grant Deed To Transfer A Fee Simple Ownership To A New Buyer.
- A Condition Subsequent Agreement.
- A Use Of Fee Simple Executory Limitation, A Determinable Fee.
- Two Separate Legal Contractual Standings In The Same Investment For The CI. There Are: 1. Article Of Partnership 2. Performance Trust Deed.

Five legal positions are granted to the CI in the LP, they are:

- Limited Partner.
- Grant Deed.
- Performance Trust Deed.
- Priority Use Privilege.
- Collateral System.

The legal structure for the CI arranged in the EIT is a new exceptional and original grouping of legal statues and regulations. The CI is given a special legal position that afford maximum protection in the LP. The CI has two legal standings in the investment. The Articles of Partnership is a legal binding contact with terms and conditions that favor the CI's. Also, the CI receives a Performance Trust Deed that is a legal standing outside of the LP. These two legal standings give control of collateral collection in case of an LP default. These two, first-time-ever, separate CI legal contractual standings solidify the investment legal statutory standing for the CI.

LP LOSS ISSUE

<u>CI is insulated</u>. In a LP it is a fact that the limited partner is limited to losing only the amount invested by law. In the case of the CI loss of capital the CI takes title to a fee absolute ownership of property offered as collateral, that has a substantial equity. The LP is required to pass the title of ownership to the CI, if the CI funds are exhausted without a property sale occurring.

There is no foreclosure or bankruptcy possible for the CI to be involved in that would stall collection of the collateral. The cash investor has two separate legal documents to exercise the collection of the collateral pledged, the Articles of Partnership and the Performance Trust Deed. Both have contractual legal standing to collect. At the point of a default <u>the LP has absolutely no reason not to give over the title to the CI as required in the Articles.</u>

IN THE LP THERE IS NO LOAN INVOLVED

<u>While the CI investment is like making a "loan" to the LP, it is not a loan</u>. The CI funds are invested as a limited partner (CI is not making a loan to the LP) in return for a pre-agreed fixed Bonus payment. No loan is "assumed" or "taken subject to" or applied for by the LP in the EIT transaction for any reason. There is no requirement or need ever for the LP to take out a loan or become responsible for an existing loan when taking in and selling foreclosure property. The LP in not buying the property.

PROFESSIONAL REPORTS

A Property Appraisal, Construction Review Report, and the Preliminary Title Report are provided to the CI to make the investment decision. Professional reports are used to analyze and approve the first property going into the LP. The following information is given to the CI so that the CI can make an informed decision as to whether to approve the property to be used as the CI collateral? The investor approval or rejection is based on three professional reports plus a visit to the property if desired. No investor approval means no commitment to invest. An amount of net equity greater than the CI funds and the amount of Bonus added together, would be a good guideline to financially qualify the property as collateral. The appraisal will help in this regard.

Tax, Insurance, Transfer, Ownership, And Market Explanation

When devising the Extraordinary Investment Transaction, it became clear that the answer to solving all these points lie in establishing a new legal combination of current statutes and regulations to achieve the required legal, financial, and investment results needed to create the EIT.

Owners Tax Position

The owner makes a capital contribution of the property to the LP that creates a limited partner investment position in the LP. When a property is invested the appraisal amount equals a stepped-up cost basis for tax purposes. Any profit over the cost basis earned is taxable and payable at the time the LP collects income from the investment.

Property Transfer

A "Bare Title" is used to transfer a <u>dual ownership</u> between the property owner in foreclosure and the LP. The LP takes the property "Title" to hold and dispose of according to the LP Articles. The owner retains an "Equitable Interest" in the property until it is sold by the LP.

Property Insurance

The current owner of the property in foreclosure has title insurance on the property in foreclosure. Upon transfer of the title the insurance remains in effect as the owner retains legal ownership as an "equitable interest" owner. Therefore, the title insurance does not change hands until the full property ownership is sold by the LP, a new insurance policy is taken out by the new purchaser.

A Type Of Ownership Position

The equitable ownership position of the owner requires the owner to maintain the property, pay the mortgage payments, and leave the property when it is sold. The LP has the title to the property to hold until the LP sells the property at which time the LP transfers the fee simple absolute title to the new owner.

The Property Market Value

The nice thing for the foreclosure owner is that when the property's foreclosure is cured a Broker can list a foreclosure free property and achieve a full value sale. <u>History over many decades tells us when a property is in foreclosure the market value is usually the loan value plus a few thousand dollars.</u> Buyers always offers the lowest amount possible!

Investor's Status

The CI in the LP/EIT is more secured, rewarded, and safer than in other standard LP investments in all categories. The EIT investor position in the LP is designed and structured for CI success.

CHAPTER 8
VIEWING THE LIMITED PARTNERSHIP IN DIFFERENT WAYS

"ORIGINAL CREATIONS" WERE NECESSARY

These items have been created for the first time. These individual parts of a unique plan of operation working together provide exceptional results. No other transaction has the structure or performance ability of the LP/EIT. The same purpose and results of the LP/EIT have never been duplicated. To create the LP/EIT transaction in the LP:

- A LP special purpose Articles of Partnership had to established for the LP.
- A new Financial Support Plan is established to create a safe investment in a LP.
- A sale under duress had to be eliminated and a full property value sale created.
- A new Debt to Asset Ratio formula is established that lowers the CI risk.
- A new use of a Performance Trust Deed was established.
- A new default collection system for cash investor is created to ensure the investor will receive the collateral if it becomes necessary.
- A separation by creating two classes of LP limited partners was created.
- A new use for a Bare Title of ownership status (a trustee type ownership) was established in the LP agreement, that includes a no cost title transfer to the LP.
- Many millions of investment dollars can now be gathered into an O&IF in an LP from rescuing equities for the owners to invest in various profit enterprises.

There are additional techniques and procedures that are not found in any other investment transaction. "LP new EIT creation list":

- LP form of payment (a Bonus).
- New Tenant In Common ability.
- LP cash stands acts as additional collateral.
- First-time fast recourse to collect capital & Bonus, if necessary.
- Full value sale for foreclosure property.
- Unqualified owners made into qualified investors.
- LP low-risk high-return paradigm.
- LP pays the investor Bonus.
- Investor chooses collateral.
- LP reinvestment acceleration plan.
- Two Different Type Partner Roles.
- New-Different Partner Rewards.

LP MAJOR "OPERATING" IMPROVEMENTS

In the LP EIT there are many unique accomplishments in the LP:

- How to cure a foreclosure in a new way totally for the owner's benefit.
- A full value sale for a property that was in foreclosure.
- A way to rescue equity for owners from loss to a foreclosure.
- A secured transaction within a LP for a CI.
- A legal grouping working in combination to protect the CI.
- A Financial Support Plan to ensure enough time/money to sell property.
- A way to pay a CI with a pre-agreed fixed amount Bonus is created.
- A new CI risk reward opportunity that exceeds expectations.
- A new LP Debt To Asset Ratio formula that creates LP CI safety.
- Two chance success opportunity for the CI.
- A CI investment acceleration technique.
- A method for a financially insolvent owner to become a qualified investor.
- A new use for the Performance Trust Deed.
- A way to eliminate standard foreclosure investment risks in a LP.
- A new LP/EIT physical and financial structure.

WHAT THE CI KNOWS

- The CI knows there is a financial plan in place to support the property until it sells.
- The CI knows former owner now a tenant until the property sells is a partner with a strong interest in maintaining the property to ensure the highest price in the market.
- The CI knows the LP will list the property for sale immediately. The Articles dictate that the property be offered for sale immediately by the LP, as agreed by the owner.
- The CI knows there will be enough net sales proceeds to pay the Bonus.
- The CI knows the CI funds invested creates a Financial fund to operate the LP.
- The CI knows exactly what the CCC will be spent on ahead of time.
- The CI knows ahead of time the exact fixed amount of the Bonus will be.
- The CI knows the collateral protecting the CCC will increase after each LP sale.
- The CI knows the value of the property acting as collateral will be maintained.
- The CI knows the CCC will be returned in full before LP investing for profit begins.
- The CI knows the true property physical condition and legal status of the property.
- The CI knows there is no cash reserve required to back-up invested funds.
- The CI knows that the limited partners do not control the money invested or the property title or are they able to make any LP decisions.
- The CI knows that the transaction is expense free.

- The CI knows that legally the CI will be separate from other partners.
- The CI knows the owner take all the financial risk of the LP investments.
- The CI knows if the owner pays the full rent the LP will not use any of the CCC.
- The CI knows the investment money is replenished after each LP property sale before a new property is taken into the LP.
- The CI knows there is an early return of capital privilege and will exit the LP after three LP property sales are made, estimated to take one year!
- The CI knows there is no foreclosure or bankruptcy concern that affects the CI.
- The CI knows there is an ability to oversee spending by the LP of the CI funds invested. Allowable LP expenditures: To immediately cure the subject property foreclosure, to prepare the property for sale by the LP, to pay any escrow closing costs to transfer the title to the LP, to support the monthly loan(s) payments on the property, if necessary.
- The CI knows the property owner will leave the property upon sale when asked. The owner wants to complete the transaction and rescue all the equity. A penalty for not moving on time would lower the rescued amount by several thousand dollars.

THE CI SHOULD KNOW WHAT DOES NOT HAPPEN IN THE LP/EIT

- NO sale or (purchase) takes place between the owner of property and the LP.
- NO profit is earned on the property in foreclosure by the LP.
- NO money is given for the title to the foreclosure property by the LP.
- NO expense is charged to the CI or the owner by the LP.
- NO money is given directly to the owner in foreclosure by the CI, GP, or the LP.
- NO profit is earned by the LP when it sells and collects the net sales proceeds from the property contributed by the owner in foreclosure.
- NO promise is every made to the foreclosure owner that he/she will receive any money/profit from the LP until dissolution of the LP.
- NO profit will be distributed to the limited partners until all the startup and operating expenses of the LP have been deducted and paid first.
- NO investment for profit will begin until the CI is paid and leaves the Partnership.
- NO foreclosure or bankruptcy that would involve the cash investor is possible.
- NO other personal debts of the foreclosure owners enter the transaction.

CHAPTER 9
LP GENERAL OPERATION REVIEW

CONSIDERATION <u>GIVEN</u> BY THE OWNER IN THE PARTNERSHIP AGREEMENT

The owner agrees to:

1. Use the property in foreclosure as collateral to secure the cash investor's funds.
2. Favor the cash investors with financial and investment advantages.
3. Become an investor in the LP, using the sales proceeds of the property rescued from foreclosure, when the LP sells the property.
4. To invest in investments to be made by the LP.
5. The owner agrees to take all the financial risk of and in the LP.

CONSIDERATION <u>RECEIVED</u> BY THE OWNER IN THE LP AGREEMENT

The owner immediately receives relief because the following takes place as soon as the owner joins the LP:

1. The foreclosure is cured immediately by the LP as promised by the LP.
2. The property is put up of sale by the LP immediately per owners' instructions.
3. An LP Financial Support Plan is put in place to ensure time to sell property.
4. Potential lawsuit for collection of a debt is avoided instead the debt gets paid.
5. Loan relief is achieved for the owner when the LP sells the property.
6. Time is granted to the owner to reestablish his/her financial position.
7. The use of an exclusive real estate plan is given to the owner.
8. The equity rescue earns interest and profit from the LP.
9. All negative consequences of a foreclosure are resolved for the owner.
10. The owner has found a way to join a financially sound group that immediately makes an insolvent owner into a qualified real estate investor.

CONSIDERATION <u>GIVEN</u> BY THE CI IN THE LP AGREEMENT

The CI agrees to:

1. Invest in the same partnership with financially insolvent partners.
2. Approve the first property to be contributed to the LP.
3. Invest $60,000 in the LP to be used to cure three property foreclosures and to support the property loans on each property, if necessary, until all three properties are sold. This fund allows the LP to offer the property for sale at "arm's length" to obtain the fair market value for the property. The CI eliminates all the financial and emotional duress caused by the ongoing foreclosure for the owner.
4. Accept, if necessary, the property fee simple ownership title as collateral, to replace

the CI funds invested if the LP uses all the funds without achieving a property sale.

CONSIDERATION RECEIVED BY THE CI IN THE LP AGREEMENT

The CI receives:

1. An investment, the terms of which cannot be altered or change by the other partners in the LP at any time.
2. A choice and approval of the collateral to be used as the security.
3. A sufficient collateral made up of property and LP cash on hand that increases in amount as each property sale is completed by the LP.
4. Five (5) legal positions working in combination that provide a high degree of safety.
5. A pre-agreed amount of Bonus earned and secured immediately upon providing the investment funds to the startup LP escrow.
6. No necessity to earn profit through a risky investment venture as the Bonus is paid from existing equities when three properties are sold.
7. Acknowledgement that each property taken into the LP will be offered for sale immediately according to the Articles of Partnership agreement.
8. A favored safety and financial position over all other LP partners.
9. An early return of capital and payment of a secured pre-agreed amount of Bonus.
10. An agreement that the CI fund be replenished after each LP sale.
11. A Bonus acceleration opportunity at the completion of each LP.

CONSIDERATION GIVEN BY THE GP IN THE PARTNERSHIP AGREEMENT

1. The expertise to accomplish the purposes of all the partners.
2. The willingness to take on responsibility for the results.
3. The personal time to oversee all LP activities.
4. The providing of the exclusive plan for all the other limited partners.
5. To complete an expense free investment for all its partners.
6. To direct investments to achieve earning for the partners.

CONSIDERATION RECEIVED BY THE GP IN THE PARTNERSHIP AGREEMENT

1. The biggest and only opportunity the GP gets from managing the LP is the fact that the GP has investment oversight of a very large ever-growing investment fund. There will be several fees that can be earned by operating this investment. In addition, the GP receives a salary and a share of the profits from the LP.
2. The LP can create new and valuable real estate transactions that could not be accomplished without the use of the EIT in the LP.

The LP Duties And Operation:

1. The LP takes in as a tax deferred capital contribution a property that is in

foreclosure through the escrow company.

2. The LP gives to the CI a "Performance Trust Deed" to secure the pledge made to the CI in the Articles to give over the title to the property if the CI funds are exhausted, without a sale of the property occurring.

3. LP makes sure Immediately from escrow the foreclosure is cured.

4. The property is then immediately listed for sale with a real estate broker.

5. The property is sold, and the sales proceeds are invested in ventures by the LP.

NEW OPERATIONAL TECHNOLOGIES IN THE LP/EIT

1. LP/EIT has developed a new technology which allows a property owner in financial difficulty to not only rescue the property equity from foreclosure or a giveaway sale because the LP arranges a full price marketplace sale by eliminating the duress sale syndrome the owners are under while in foreclosure. All this with no financial cost to the owners to pay for the service provided.

2. LP/EIT has developed a new technology to measure the risk factor for investing in an LP. The new LP Debt To Asset Ratio (DAR) allows financing to occur to take a property out of foreclosure when no other financial answer works safely enough to proceed to make the investment of new funds in the property.

3. LP/EIT has created a new LP technology designed just to accomplish (1) and (2) above. This LP has many advantages for all the partners participating in it. Some so unique that they have never been though of or accomplished before and are going to lead the way in the future when it comes to real estate passive investment.

4. LP/EIT has developed a new technology to ensure the return of invested capital along with the financial reward promised by the LP to the investor regardless of the performance or non-performance of LP.

5. LP/EIT has developed a new technology that of self-generating large sums of operating and investment capital quickly which will become real estate venture capital to invest for profit and help the owners earn and build their new financial position. This would allow the partners to return as buyers to the real estate marketplace within a much shorter period then if the owners lost the equity to foreclosure or to a foreclosure speculator.

6. LP/EIT has developed a new technology that allows the LP to interact in new and powerful ways that no other real estate legal entity can duplicate or perform. This

technology makes all foreclosure property procurement and LP investment for profit safer than current real estate can arrange or obtain.

7. LP/EIT has developed a new technology by which a new risk vs. reward opportunity is created in the marketplace that is outstanding when compared to what is available in the real estate industry.

8. LP/EIT has a new "financial advancement of funds" ability. It is a new way to fund money to cure a foreclosure in process when the property has reached the maximum equity borrowing limit of 65% to 70% LTV.

SPECIAL PURPOSE REQUIREMENTS INCORPORATED IN AN LP/EIT

Incorporated in the LP are the following unique structures that introduce and achieve new ways for a LP to operate and perform for its partners and at the same time solve a very difficult and harmful societal problem.

- Structured a special way to attract money safely from a cash investor that will provide the money needed to rescue property equity from foreclosure and make it grow in amount.

- Structured a way to add cash to the total asset amount while the property asset is still in foreclosure and by doing so created a Debt to Asset Ratio that creates a cash and property combination. This cash infusion improves the safety factor for the cash investor because it features both a property title of ownership and reserve cash acting as collateral in the investment. This ability to attract cash into the investment creates a unique and very safe investment for the investor.

- Structured two different classes of limited partners, with different financial qualifications, rewards, and role responsibilities, in the same . This structure allows for the first time in a financially insolvent investor to be in the same LP together with a qualified investor without having any legal or financial entanglements with each other.

- Structured and created a unique secured Bonus reward payment system for a qualified cash investor. A Bonus is secured at the start of the LP, for just one investor in the LP. The Bonus is a pre-agreed fixed amount and is initially paid out of property sales without the LP required to make a dime in profits to pay the investor Bonus.

64

- Structured a secured transaction within a LP for just one limited partner, while at the same time creating a safe investment for all the other limited partners in the same LP.

- Structured security for the cash investor's money by securing a LP pledge made in the Articles of Partnership Agreement. Behind the pledge stands collateral, approved by the cash investor, in the form of a fee simple absolute real property title of ownership.

- Structured a "Financial Support Plan" that uses a Critical Cash Capital fund that ensures payment of the current mortgage payments on property taken out of foreclosure, if necessary, so that the property will not go back into a foreclosure process. The payment plan creates enough time to expose the property in the open market so that a full value sale can be made, and the equity can be rescued.

- Structured several legal positions created for just one limited partner in a LP, that affords the limited partner investing cash in the LP, unequaled financial protection in an investment transaction.

- Structured a system of increasing the cash investor's original collateral amount that protects the cash investor's funds. A system that adds cash collateral and increases the collateral amount, after the LP has started.

- Structured a way to generate and harness millions of dollars of LP operational and investment funds by helping property owners rescue their entire property equity from foreclosure.

- Structured a way to obtain a full value sale for a property in the foreclosure process by curing the Notice of Default and eliminating the penny-on-the-dollar offers that the pressure of an ongoing foreclosure causes.

- Structured a LP that has the LP acting as a fiduciary by just holding the Bare Title, on condition, to real property transferred by the owner to the LP. The owner retains all the legal equitable rights and obligations of ownership, until the property is sold.

- Structured a LP that requires the owner whose property was rescued from foreclosure pay each month the monthly loan payments on the property either in cash or through the sale of the property.

- Structured legal and financial contractual considerations in a LP that allows one limited partner to be favored in ways that all other limited partners are not favored.

- Structured a use for a Performance Trust Deed in a new way that secures a pledge of property ownership to secure invested capital of one limited partner within a LP.

- Structured an investor collateral collection system that eliminates the need or possibility for a foreclosure or bankruptcy involving the qualified cash investor from occurring.

Structured for a property owner whose property is in the foreclosure process a way to enjoy several important advantages while avoiding the nasty consequences a foreclosure occurring would cause.

USING THE LPs OPERATING AND INVESTMENT FUND (O&IF)

As explained the Operating and Investment Fund (O&IF) is the avenue for a LP to gain investment capital to invest for the property owners turned into LP investors. This fund will grow as each LP is started and LPs can join with other LPs to share an investment position. In time the O&IF's together will amount to several millions of dollars every year to investment by the LPs. There are several unique investments and standard investment transactions with advanced performance ability created. Having a large investment capital fund on an ever-increasing yearly basis allows for creativity and safety at the same time.

LP/EIT SPIN OFF PLANS

1031 EXCHANGE PLAN

This plan will allow an exchange broker to use LP high value "cash out" properties that are for sale by the LP to exchange into. The LP will be selling high value properties to rescue the equities from foreclosure for the owners. High value cash out properties are hard to find because hardly anyone wants to pay the capital gain tax.

Having a source for the cash out property "waiting" will allow the exchanger to build up and exchange a lower priced property to the high value cash out property. The cash out property will be waiting for the exchanger to build to and close the exchange. The necessary exchange property needed to exchange up to the high value "cash out" property is in the LP waiting to be sold.

PORTFOLIO ADJUSTMENT

Portfolio Property Plan

Many millions of investors throughout the United States have four or five properties in their residential investment portfolio. The LP/EIT can solve a portfolio negative cash flow problem that drags down the portfolio positive cash flow. The LP/EIT can take in the property that has negative cash flow and leave the investor with only the cash flowing properties. This will give more cash income from the portfolio cash flowing properties and help the owner's financial standing and credit standing.

The native cash flow property's Bare Title transferred to the LP will become an investment made by the owner in the LP. The same as when a foreclosure is transferred to the LP. The property will be sold and the property's revenue from sale will be credited to the owner's capital account and continue earning a profit share. Tax will be deferred until the investor receives profit from the LP.

CHAPTER 10
CLOSING REMARKS

》》QUESTION 1:

How can a property owner, who cannot cure a pending property foreclosure, have the foreclosure cured and avoid all the nasty financial consequences a foreclosure will cause?

The LP/EIT is the "only way" to arrange for the owner a fair and honest financial answer.

》》QUESTION 2:

Where is a legally safe and secure investment found that pays a fixed minimum reward of $25,500 to a maximum of $42,500 in about a year, with no personal investor time or legal liability?

This question "exactly describes" what the CI receives in the LP/EIT.

》》QUESTION 3:

How are extraordinarily large sums of investment capital accumulated on a repetitive never-ending basis to safely invest in real estate ventures accomplished? The LP/EIT transaction will raise a large amount of investment capital, one amount at a time, in each foreclosure cured and sold at full value. This is a "advanced way" to gather capital to invest, the O&IF is an original first-time achievement. Innovative real estate investments and real estate financial transactions of all kinds can now take place because of the LP/EIT.

NOTES:

Every investor wants the best financial and legal position along with a timely reward. I think most would agree that the LP/EIT meets this vision and that it is a very best investment design. The CI is happy to receive all the investment benefits and individual legal support the LP/EIT offers.

The LP/EIT can advance funds to cure owner's property foreclosure when no one else would or could. It provides a better safer way to invest in all types of real estate, not just foreclosures. It can solve many difficult real estate financial problems for the first time.

Real estate brokers, investors, lenders, and property owners substantially gain financially from the LP's ability to create safe more rewarding investments. The LP/LP is a major accomplishment in many ways.

What is the most sensitive point that allows the LP/EIT to operate? It is the need of the owner who, because of a strong financial need, will join and cooperate in the participation of every critical aspect of the LP/EIT.

The key requirement to making the LP/EIT work is how the legal problem was solved. The legal combination that is used to allow the transaction to occur is paramount to achieving the desired result. This legal combination has never been used for this purpose before. Without the new legal combination, the LP/EIT cannot happen. It is true while people involved need to co-operate and agree to their individual role, it is the legal structure that is so new and allows the LP/EIT to be formed and operate.

Wishing you the best,
Robert L. Evans
r.leeevans@aol.com

www.ingramcontent.com/pod-product-compliance
Lightning Source LLC
Chambersburg PA
CBHW041124120626
46547CB00019B/2838